TURKEY

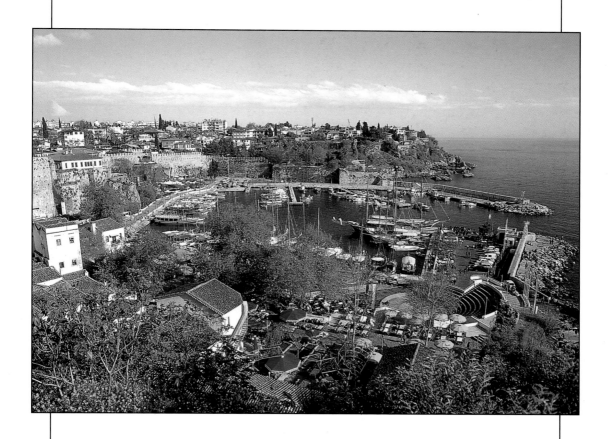

R E V A Ş
REHBER BASIM YAYIN DAĞITIM
REKLAMCILIK VE TİCARET A.Ş.

REVAK

TURKEY

Published and Distributed by
REVAŞ Rehber Basım Yayın Dağıtım
Reklamcılık ve Tic. A.Ş.

Photos :
Erdal Yazıcı, Şemsi Güner, Selâmet Taşkın,
Güngör Özsoy, Halûk Özözlü, Tahsin Aydoğmuş,
Firdevs Sayılan, Dönence Diabank.

Graphic and Layout :
Kemal Özdemir

Typsetting :
AS & 64 Ltd. Şti.

Colour Separation and Printed Turkey by
Çali Grafik Matbaacılık A.Ş.

ISBN 975-8212-06-0

R E V A Ş
REHBER BASIM YAYIN DAĞITIM
REKLAMCILIK VE TİCARET A.Ş.

İnönü Mahallesi, Ölçek Sokak No: 172-174,
Harbiye, İstanbul-TURKEY
Tel: (90-212) 240 72 84 - 240 58 05
Fax: (90-212) 231 33 50

REVAK
TURKEY

CONTENTS

WELCOME TO TURKEY

Visiting for the first time? You may say yes or no, but you sure know this country. Let us guide you through the history and mythology; you will find out, you know this country, you know it very well indeed..

As you travel east from the birthplace of Alexander the Great, you will approach Thrace, the northwestern territory of Turkey, and here, you will hear the most captivating music of

a world of dreams with Sappho's verses that echoes from the island of Lesbos, right across.

Further south, as you reach Ionia, you greet the people of Phokaia, founders of Marseilles and search for gold powder in the Paktolos river as you watch the seals dance to the cries of the sirens.

You taste the world-famous figs in Izmir, named after the Amazon Queen, Smyrna, and the city where Homer was born. You reach Teos; and as Plato and Apellikon revise their works, they cast a sharp look on you; "lousy tourists!".

Boğazköy, Yazılıkaya, Hittite Sacred Area, Relief of 12 gods.

Orpheus. As you approach Asia by crossing the choppy waters of the Dardanelles Strait, you see the silhouette of Leander, swimming across the strait every night to his beloved. At a distance, the Achean craftsmen are building the legendary Trojan horse; and over the walls of Troy, Paris and Hector are sadly watching the bay where Agamemnon's ships were once anchored. Not far away, the Amazon Queen Pantelia is in a fierce fight against Achilles, the hero.

Heading south to Assos, you will be relieved by the fresh Aeolian wind on the terrace of Plato's school and you get into

You continue on your journey to Ephesus and there it is; the Temple of Artemis, one of the seven wonders of the ancient world.

You listen to Heraclitus as he delivers his speech in the Odeon; or attend the crowd as St. Paul preaches in the largest theater of the ancient times and you witness his efforts to spread Christianity.

Way up Mount Koressos, you reach the House of Virgin Mary and back in Ephesus, you visit the apostle John as he writes his Gospel. Next city is Miletus, the capital for positive sciences; and here, you get to know the reputable

Istanbul Hippodrome, Detail of obelisk base reliefs.

philosophers of the ancient past; Thales, Pythagoras, Anaximenes, Anaximander...

In Priene, you witness the great achievement of the urban planner, Hippodamus: the first application of the grid plan. You take your time to listen to Goddess Athena. At the temple in Didyma, you ask the question on your mind to God Apollo: "Will there ever be a universal peace?".

You travel south and you are in the Karian territory. Right before your eyes is one other wonder of the ancient world; The Mausoleum of Halicarnassos, monumental burial for the Persian Satrap for their affair. You travel east, along the coastline, to Aspendos; and here, in the best preserved theater of the ancient times, the great architect Zenon waits for you to show you his masterpiece. Further east to Tarsus; you take a look at the house where St. Paul was born and continue to Antioch, the birthplace of Peter, to visit the world's most popular mosaic museum and the church of St. Peter.

As you cross the river Euphrates, you reach upper Mesopotamia; then you go way up Mt. Nemrut and witness the incredible outcome of the obsessions of

Istanbul, Hagia Sophia Museum.

Istanbul, Bosphorus Bridge.

Mausolus. En route to Aphrodisias, you stop by Nyssa and visit the renowned geographer Strabon as a young scholar in the school. As you gaze at the school of sculpture in Aphrodisias, you realize that the young trainees are the future sculptors of the Roman Empire, to create exceptional works of art with great skill. As you pass by Myra, you stop to visit Santa Claus and light a candle in the church. You reach Phaselis; this should be the paradise!. Now you see why Alexander the Great spent the whole winter here, or why Anthony and Cleopatra had chosen this particular spot

the Commagene King, Antiochus. Giant statues of gods and the awesome tumulus are still in situ and awaits the visitors.

You travel down south to Urfa and take a sip from the cold water in the cave of Prophet Abraham. Harran is also nearby and the Temple of Sin is definitely worth a visit.

Welcome to Turkey...

With an approximate area of 780,000 km2 and over 65 million population, Turkey is one of the most interesting countries in our aged world. Throughout the history of mankind, Turkey, for its unique location, has always been an ideal

site for many civilizations and many left their traces as they passed through. Almost all scholars agree that Turkey is "the world's largest open-air museum". A bridge between East and West, North and South, and Asia and Europe; Turkey is definitely one of the most attractive countries on earth.

From the earliest human settlements, dated back to the Paleolithic era (8.000 BC), the continuous progress of mankind can be traced through the Neolithic, Calcolithic eras to the Bronze and Iron ages. The excavations carried out in hundreds of ancient sites throughout the country, are the evidences of a great culture, from the Hittites to Phrigians and Urartians; Lydians to Persians and Achaeans. A country of unrivaled heritage, "the Cradle of Civilizations".

Turkey, a huge country with a touch of Mediterranean culture and more; the country of tolerance, and of warm, hospitable people who could share the last loaf of bread with a stranger that knocks on the door.

Turkey, the country of caring people, people that welcome any guest with generosity. A mosaic of beliefs, customs, traditions and nomad culture of the Central Asian steppes; outcome of thousands of years, blended in with the local cultures and civilizations. A country that belongs to the proud descendants of a great past.

A country waiting to be explored; Welcome to Turkey.

GEOGRAPHY OF TURKEY

The Republic of Turkey is centrally located within the territories of the pre war Ottoman Empire that extended from the Adriatic Sea all the way to the Persian Gulf and Indian Ocean. A greater portion of Turkey is in the Asian continent and known as "Anatolia" or "Asia Minor". North-west corner of Turkey, "Eastern Thrace", occupies 23.000 km2 and is part of Europe.There is a constant increase in the elevation toward east that is

Artvin, Kaçkar Mountains, Demirkapı Peak.

Konya, Meke Crater Lakee.

Fethiye, View of the Fethiye Bay.

Denizli, Pamukkale Travertines.

KARA DEN[İZ]

BULGARİSTAN
(BULGARIA)

YUNANİSTAN
(GREECE)

SİN

Svilengrad
Lalapaşa
Kofçaz
Süloğlu
KIRKLARELİ
EDİRNE
Pınarhisar
Demirköy
Havsa
Babaeski
Pehlivanköy
Lüleburgaz
Vize
Saray
Meriç
Uzunköprü
Hayrabolu
Çerkezköy
Keşan
Malkara
İSTANBUL
Çatalca
Sile
Ağva
Doğanyurt
Abana
Çatalzeytin
İnebolu
Bozkurt
Türkeli
Ayancık
Erdelek
İpsala
M.Ereğlisi
Silivri
B.Çekmece
Beykoz
Kandıra
Kurucaşile
Cide
Şenpazar
Azdavay
Ağlı
Küre
Gerze
Enez
TEKİRDAĞ
HERAKLEIA
K.Çekmece
Ümraniye
Karasu
Akçakoca
AMASTRIS
Amasra
BARTIN
Ulus
Pınarbaşı
Seydiler
Devrekani
Taşköprü
Daday
KALEKAPI
KASTAMONU
Saraydüzü
Kargı
AINOS
MARMARA DENİZİ
KOCAELİ
(İzmit)
SAKARYA
(Adapazarı)
Kaynarca
Ferizli
Kocaali
Çaycuma
Gökçebey
Eflani
Safranbolu
KARABÜK
Araç
İhsangazi
Tosya
Osmancık
Gümüş
Laçin

SAROS KÖRFEZİ
Gökçeada
Eceabat
Gelibolu
Lapseki
ABYDOS
ÇANAKKALE
KAPANBELEN
Biga
Çan
ASTYRA
TROIE
Bozcaada
Ezine
NEANDRIA
Bayramiç
Ayvacık
Edremit
İvrindi
ASSOS
Burhaniye
Havran
MELENE
PERGAMON
Bergama
Dikili
Kınık
Kırkağaç
Soma
PHOKAIA
Foça
Aliağa
KYME
Menemen
Saruhanlı
Karaburun
Çeşme
KLAZOMENAI
İZMİR
Urla
TEOS
Seferihisar
MANİSA
Turgutlu
Ahmetli
Kemalpaşa
SARDES
Salihli
Alaşehir
Ödemiş
KOLOE
Bayındır
Kiraz
Eşme
Ulubey
Banaz
UŞAK
AEZANAI
ARIANDOS
Pazarlar
Şaphane
Simav
Gördes
Demirci
Sındırgı
Akhisar
Gölmarmara
Köprübaşı
Selendi

EGE DENİZİ

Lesvos Adası
(Midilli Adası)
Midilli
Çandarlı
Çandarlı Krf.
İzmir Körfezi
Kara Ada
Chios Adası
(Sakız Adası)
Çeşme
Ildırı
Sığacık Krf.
Samos Adası
(Sisam Adası)
İkaria Adası
(Nikarya Adası)
Selçuk
EFES
İncirliova
AYDIN
Germencik
Koçarlı
Nazilli
Köşk
PRIENE
NEAPOLIS
Kuşadası
Söke
MİLET
DIDYMA
Patmos Adası
Leros Adası
Agathonisi Adası
(Eşek Adası)
Yenipazar
Karacasu
APHRODISIAS
Bozdoğan
Çine
Karpuzlu
LAGINA
Yatağan
BARKLIYA
Milas
MYNDOS
Kos Adası
(İstanköy Adası)
Bodrum
HALIKARNASSOS
KNIDOS
Datça
Ula
MUĞLA
Köyceğiz
Kavaklıdere
Kale
Beyağaç
THERA
LATONA
KAUNOS
Ortaca
Dalaman
Marmaris
Simi Adası
(Sömbeki Adası)
Tilos Adası
KADYNA
Fethiye
PINARA
XANTHOS
LETOON
PATARA
Kaş
Kale
CHIMAERA
MYRA
MEYİSTİ
(Meis Adası)
Kalkan
ARYKANDA
PHASELIS
Kumluca
Finike
Demre
Rodos
Rodhos Adası
(Rodos Adası)
Khalki Adası
(Harki Adası)

PLAKIA
Erdek
Kapıdağ Yarımadası
Paşa Adası
İmralı Adası
Bandırma
Karacabey
APAMEIA
MILETOPOLIS
Gönen
Manyas
M.Kemal Paşa
Orhaneli
Susurluk
Balya
BALIKESİR
Bigadiç
Savaştepe
Kepsut
Dursunbey
Harmancık
Emet
Hisarcık
Çavdarhisar
KÜTAHYA
Tavşanlı
ASLANKAYA
KAPIKAYA
Aslanapa
Han
Altıntaş
İhsaniye
AFYON
Sincanlı
Dumlupınar
Hocalar
Sivaslı
Karahallı
Çivril
Kızılören
Şuhut
Çobanlar
Çay
Bolvadin
PESSINUS
Günyüzü
Emirdağ
Çeltik
Kulu

MARMARA DENİZİ
YALOVA
Altınova
Karamürsel
Gölcük
Çınarcık
Armutlu
Termal
Orhangazi
Sapanca
Akyazı
Karapürçek
Geyve
Söğütlü
Hendek
Gölyaka
Düzce
BOLU
Yeniçağa
Gerede
Çerkeş
Dörtdivan
Mudurnu
Seben
Çamlıdere
GANGRA
ÇANKIRI
Orta
Kızılcahamam
Eldivan
Şabanözü
Çubuk
Uğurludağ
ÇOR[UM]
Bayat

BURSA
Kestel
Gürsu
Mudanya
Gemlik
NICAEA
İznik
Yenişehir
İnegöl
Pazaryeri
Osmaneli
Gölpazar
Gömeç
Tarakli
Göynük
Nallıhan
Beypazarı
Kazan
Ayaş
Sincan
Etimesgut
ANKARA
Elmadağ
Balışeyh
KIRIKKALE
Delice
YOZGAT
Yerköy
Akçakent
Çiçekdağı
Kaman
Boztepe
Yenifakı
Kozaklı
KIRŞEHİR
Mucur
Hacıbektaş
Avanos
ÜRGÜP
Gülşehir
NEVŞEHİR
Acıgöl
Derinkuyu

BİLECİK
İnhisar
Mihalgazi
Sarıcakaya
Bozüyük
Mihalıçcık
İnönü
ESKİŞEHİR
Alpu
Beylikova
GORDION
Mahmudiye
Seyitgazi
Sivrihisar
Çifteler
Polatlı
Haymana
GAVURKALE
Bahçeli
Bala
Karakeçili
Keskin
Kırıkkale
Çelebi
Şefaatli
TUZ GÖLÜ
Cihanbeyli
Şereflikoçhisar
Evren
Sarıyahşi
Ağaçören
Ortaköy
Gülağaç
ACEMHÜYÜK
AKSARAY
IHLARA
Güzelyurt
Ciftlik
Altınhisar
NİĞDE
TYANA
Bor
Çam[ardı]
Kazanhüyük
Yalvaç
Akşehir
Sarayönü
Sarıkaraağaç
İlgın
Derbent
Kadınhanı
Altınekin
Emirgazi
Karapınar
Ereğli
Ulukışla
Pozantı
Kar[aisalı]
Halkapınar
KARAMAN
Çamlıyayla

BURDUR
ISPARTA
Ağlasun
KREMNA
Bucak
Eğirdir
Aksu
Yenişarbademli
Şarkikaraağaç
Gelendost
Senirkent
Uluborlu
Dinar
Gönen
Keçiborlu
Atabey
Başmakcı
Hüyük
Beyşehir
Seydişehir
Derebucak
KONYA
Çumra
Gökhöyük
Ahırlı
Bozkır
Güneysınır
Kazımkarabekir
Ayrancı
Hadım
Taşkent
İbradı
Akseki
Gündoğmuş
Ermenek
Mut
ALAHAN
KANLIDİVANE
Erdemli
YAMUKTEPE
VİRANŞEHİR
İÇEL
(Mersin)
KIZKALESI
CENNET
CEHENNEM
AYATEKLA
Silifke
Gülnar
Aydıncık
Anamur
Bozyazı
ANAMURYUM

DENİZLİ
Buldan
Buharkent
PAMUKKALE
Güney
Bekilli
Çal
Baklan
Çardak
Dazkırı
Bozkurt
Honaz
Serinhisar
Tavas
Yeşilova
Acıpayam
Karamanlı
Kemer
Tefenni
Çavdır
OLBASA
Gölhisar
Çameli
Altınyayla
Elmalı
Korkuteli
SELGE
PERGE
SILLYON
TERMESSOS
Serik
ASPENDOS
SIDE
ANTALYA
Manavgat
Manavgat Şelalesi
ALARAHAN
Gazipaşa
Alanya
Antalya Körfezi

AK DENİZ

K.K.T.C
(T.R.N.C)
GİRNE
GÜZELYURT
LEFKOŞA
GAZİMAĞUSA
GAZİBAF
LARNAKA
LİMASOL

interrupted by the Central Anatolian Plateau, at around 800 m. above sea level. Further east, the elevation reaches an average of 2000-2200 m. The Taurus mountain range, with an average elevation of 2500 m. (peaks 4000 m.) , extends along the Mediterranean coast line and dominates the southern part of Turkey. The Pontic chain in the north has an average elevation of 1500 m. (reaches 3600 m . toward east) and lies parallel to the Black Sea. The mountain ranges of Western Anatolia lie on east-west axis, vertical to the Aegean Sea. This situation has created an extremely irregular coast line, embroidered with natural wonders, amazing bays and peninsulas.

In the south, rivers, fed by the snow water down from the peaks of the Taurus mountains, irrigate many fertile plains of the Mediterranean coast, rich with alluvial soil. The plateaus to the east of the tectonic basin of the Salt Lake are dominated by several volcanoes with a height of 3000 m. to 4000 m. and higher. Mt. Ararat (5165 m. elevation) is the highest of these volcanoes. Located in the same region, Lake Van (3600 km2), is the largest lake of the country.

The wide plains of Eastern Anatolia, essentially, are most suitable for cattle farming; whereas, the lower valleys and plains (such as the fertile Iğdır Plain) are cultivated to a certain extend. The two major sources of water, Euphrates and Tigris rivers, originate in this region and flow south as the elevation constantly drops. They irrigate South-East Anatolian region known as Upper Mesopotamia and leave Turkey.

As one approaches north toward the Black Sea, it is seen that the mountain ranges, in general, extend very close to the water. As a result, the coastline is dominated by mountains that sharply decline down toward the sea and only a few plains of alluvial soil (such as Bafra

Anatolian Population.
Muğla, Young girls on national holiday.
Malatya, copper smiths in copper market.
Sinop, local musicians at traditional wedding party.

and Çarşamba) are observed.

Thrace and Anatolian districts around the Sea of Marmara consists of large, comparatively flat lands of fertile soil, crowned by only a few peaks.

CLIMATE AND VEGETATION

A large portion of Turkey is influenced by the Mediterranean climate. Therefore, the summer months are warm and dry and the winter is mild and rainy. There are significant changes in seasonal and day and night temperatures. The Black Sea coast, especially the eastern portion, gets the highest rainfall.

The Central and East Anatolian Plateaus are semi barren and has scarce vegetation. Large areas of poplar trees are common along the rivers. Throughout the ages, there has been a huge consumption and destruction of forests and the severe results of land erosion are clearly visible. However, the mountain ranges that border these plateaus has some dense vegetation and large forested regions with a rich variety of trees. The southern part of the country basically has vast areas of low bushes and shrubs.

Turkey can not be considered a rich country in terms of underground waters and rivers as a result of land characteristics and unsuitable climate conditions. None of the rivers are suitable for navigation and transportation.

DEMOGHRAPHY

The estimated population of Turkey is well over 65 million. The 3 million citizens, currently living in foreign countries, especially in Germany, should also be taken into account. Today, 70% of the population reside in towns and cosmopolitan cities and the rest, in rural areas. After 1950's, the structural changes in the society, mechanization in agriculture and industrial progress have resulted in an extensive displacement of

Bozcaada, a coffeehouse on the shore.
Erdek, fishermen.
Assos, young kilim seller.

11

regional populations. The outcome of this internal immigration is still a serious issue on the agenda; shacks in the big city ghettos and poverty. From 1960's on, the high birth-rate that resulted in a very young population, has been taken under control by intensive family planning programs and birth control.

In Turkey today, a vast majority of the population lives in the Aegean, Mediterranean and primarily in the Marmara regions, far more developed compared to the East and South-East Anatolian regions that currently has severe economical problems.

HISTORY OF ANATOLIA

The earliest traces of mankind in Asia Minor date back to the Upper Paleolithic era, roughly 100.000 BC.. Excavations, carried out in several major sites, provided important clues on a number of substantial human settlements from 8.000 BC on. Çayönü (7.250-6.750 BC) and Hacılar (7.040 BC) are both dated to the aceramic age. The Catalhoyuk settlement (6.500-5.650 BC), with twelve subsequent levels discovered so far, stands out as a most distinguished center of prehistoric culture and demonstrates the first systematic urban settlement (an estimated population of 5 to 10 thousand) recorded in history. Can Hasan (5.500 BC on) to the first settlement in Troy (correspond to 3.000 BC.), Anatolia falls into a dark age with almost no remarkable progress over the dominant rural culture. The early Bronze Age marks an important break-through for the history of Anatolia. In the second half of the 3rd millennium BC., the Hattic culture, that existed throughout the Asia Minor, represent the summit of the Bronze Age civilization. The Hattic people created a unique civilization, outside of Mesopotamia, with the notion of being a nation in the real sense. The commercial and cultural relations between Anatolia and Mesopotamia, from the Akkadians (2.350 BC.) to the late

Assyrian Kingdom (8thcen. BC.), also starts at this very same age. The cultural interaction of Troy-II civilization in the west and central Anatolian cultures is remarkable. As the new layers of settlements succeed one another in Troy (III-V., 2.200-1.800 BC.), the Hattic culture vanishes and gives way to the Hittites. This transition age marks the beginning of written history in Anatolia. The Assyrian Trade Colonies, established in Kanesh (Kültepe) and some other sites, represent the extension of the Mesopotamian civilization in Asia Minor.

HITTITES (18th-12thcen. BC.): The Hittites, throughout the Old Kingdom, had a weak and decentralized administration. Based on the earlier efforts, they reunited and established the Hittite Empire that shows an excellent central organization and made Hattusa (Boğazköy) their capital city. In the 15th and 14thcen. BC., the Hittites enlarged their territories, to the Sea of Marmara in the west and towards the states along the Euphrates in the east, fighting against the Hurrians, Mitanni Empire and the barbarian Keskas of the Pontic region. They signed the first peace treaty (Kadesh, 1.285 BC.) of the world history at the end of the war against the Egyptians, under the reign of Ramses II., for the control of Syria. The last phase of the Hittite history is patterned by the decentralization of the government. The city states, established as a result, survived till the 7thcen. BC. The remains of the Hittite civilization, certainly the most influential of the historic ages in Anatolia, have survived to our time in many substantial sites (Hattuşa, Yazılıkaya, Alacahöyük, Malatya, Karkamish, Sakcagözü, Zincirli, Karatepe, etc.) with numerous works of art and architecture, created with great skill.

URARTIANS AND PHRYGIANS: As the Hittites gradually disappeared from the scene of history by the turn of the last millennium before Christ, a new civilization came into existence, in the

Konya, Ereğli, Ivriz reliefs, Hittite, King Warpawalas pays homage to Tarhu, God of Abundance.

vast plateau of Lake Van in East Anatolia; the Urartians. Considered as the descendants of the Hurrians, the Urartians invented sophisticated techniques in metallurgy (especially Bronze), and created a high level of civilization, observed in several sites in the region. The most significant Urartian settlements are located in Eastern Anatolia; Altıntepe, Toprakkale and Çavuştepe.

In the 13th cen. BC., the Phyrigians, of an unknown origin, came into Asia Minor over the Dardannels and the Bosphorus straits and established a great civilization in Central and North Anatolia. The earliest documents on the Phrygians are of Achean origin. The Illiad identify the Phrygians as allies of the Trojans (Anatolians) in the Trojan War. This civilization left behind thousands of valuable works of art in several sites, such as Aslankaya, Alişar, Alaca, Pazarlı

and the capital city, Gordion and disappeared with the Persian invasion, in the 6th cen. BC..

LYDIANS, LYCIANS AND CARIANS: The same age witnessed the rise of the Lycian, Lydian and Carian civilizations in West and South-West Anatolia.

Lydians and Lycians are recognized as native people of Anatolia whereas the Carians, descendants of the Lelegians, immigrated into Anatolia during the Minoan times. The capital of the Lycians, Xanthos, presents the finest artifacts of this unique civilization. Sardis, a great inspration to Greek art and architecture in Asia Minor, was the capital city of the Lydian Kingdom and the administrative center of the legendary King Croeseus. It may be uncertain that coin was first minted by the Lydians, but the city of Sardis, in the middle of the Pactolos (Gediz) valley, stood for the summit of

*Eskişehir,
King Midas
Monument, 5th
century BC..*

Kütahya,
Çavdarhisar,
Aizonai, Temple
of Zeus, 2nd
Century AD.

the Lydian civilization. Halicarnassus, the site of the monumental burial of the Persian Satrap Mausolus (the Mausoleum, one of the seven wonders of the ancient world); Aphrodisias, undoubtedly, one of the most charming and aesthetic cities on earth; Smyrna and Miletus, two of the earliest Lelegian settlements on the Aegean coast, were the important cities of the early Carian civilization.

THE ARRIVAL of THE SEA and ISLAND PEOPLE: From the 12thcen. BC. on, the invasion of Anatolia by warlike tribes, so called the "sea people" by the Egyptians, caused a great deal of unrest not only in Anatolia but in all of the Near-East.

Achaeans, Lelegians, Ionians, Aeolians, Dorians, Minoans of Crete and Mycenaeans; all came in waves, one after the other, from the rocky, barren islands of the Aegean and the Greek mainland to

the fertile plains and valleys of Anatolia. They had to pass through the Dardanneles on their way to the Black Sea and to do so, they had to pay a tribute to the Trojans. They did fight not to pay the fee, they won and they passed through the strait. Homer talks about gods, goddesses, Paris and the beautiful Helen and the legends; but we sure know that the reason of the war was the commercial concerns.

Tribes were assimilated by the locals and the cultures blended into a rich civilization. The cult of the Mother Goddess (Kybele, Kubaba) that existed throughout the ages in Anatolia, deeply influenced the newcomers. The cult of Zeus was surpassed by the Goddess Artemis in Ionia and Aphrodite in Caria. The strong belief in Virgin Mary; could it be an extension of the cult of the Mother Goddess.

The people of Anatolia achieved an extraordinary synthesis, as they adopted the culture of the newcomers and blended with what they already had.

It is not surprising that the Hellenistic civilization reached its summit in Asia Minor. Thales, Diogenes, Strabon; to name but a few. Philosophy, mathematics, geometry, astronomy, painting, sculpture, mosaic, ceramic; the superior level, attained in science and fine arts in almost all fields, is an outcome of this efficient synthesis.

PERSIAN INVASION: Toward the end of the 7th cen. BC., the Medes, conquering Mesopotamia, gave an end to the Assyrian Kingdom. After a short interval, defeated by the Persians of Achemenid origin, they faded away from the scene of the history. Early 5thcen. BC. is marked by the Persian invasion of Asia Minor. The Persians, under the rule of emperors Cryrus and Xerxes, went all the way to Greece and though they were forced to retreat after a series of battles in Marathon, Salamis and Plataea, they were sovereign in Anatolia till the second half of the 4th cen.BC.

HELLENISTIC AGE: As Alexander the Great crossed the Dardanelles and arrived in Anatolia in 334 BC., a new era of an astounding civilization started. He activated a new and greater synthesis of the East and Western cultures. Alexander the Great defeated Darius, the Persian, many times in battle fields, gave an end to the mighty Persian Empire and extended his territories all the way to India. He was worshipped in Egypt as the son of God Amon and in Persia, people prostrated before him. Established after the death of Alexander, the Pergamon Kingdom (283-133 BC.), that ruled in Ionia and Aeolia, created a high level of civilization, under the strong Greek influence and founded some of the most prestigious cities of Asia Minor, Hierapolis and Attaleia. The Pontic Kingdom of Mithridates and the land of Bithynia were under the oriental influence and created thousands of unrivaled works of art.

A great progress in art and science was achieved in the Hellenistic Age. The great architects and urban planners of the ancient times succeeded one another, and carried the already high level of intellectualism even higher. The Ionian school of architecture came into existence; outstanding temples, the Athena temple of Priene, Temple of Apollo in Didyma, etc. were constructed; well planned cities, Priene, Miletus, Teos and Magnesia were built. The cities of Ephesus and Pergamon reached their zenith. With the invention of parchment, Pergamon became one of the most important learning centers of its time with a library of 200,000 volumes.

THE ROMAN AGE: Due to the will of King Attalos III., the Pergamon Kingdom was granted to the Roman Empire in 133 BC. Defeating the Pontic King Mithridates who resisted against the Roman rule in Asia Minor, the Romans extended their boundaries all over Anatolia. They founded brand new cities, such as Iconium (Konya), Caesarea (Kayseri), Sebasteia (Sivas) as they restyled and

Ancient city of Priene, Temple of Athena.

renovated the cities like Ephesos, Miletus, Phokaia, Tarsus, Philadelphia, Thralles and Assos. Pamphilian and Lycian cities, Perge, Side, Aspendos, Kaunos, Antiphellos, Myra and Termessos enjoyed their golden ages. It is worth mentioning the contemporary Kommagene Kingdom of East Anatolia and King Antiochus (ruled 69 to 34 BC.) and his incredible burial site on Mt. Nemrut; the great tumulus, with enormous proportions.

CHRISTIANITY AND THE BYZANTINE EMPIRE: Anatolia has always been a sacred land since the biblical times. Noah's arc had landed on Mt. Ararat, Prophet Abraham lived in Edessa (Urfa) and Harran. St. Paul was born in Tarsus; he traveled throughout Anatolia and preached, to spread the word on the newborn religion. The followers of Jesus adopted the name "Christian", in the cave church of St. Peter in Antioch and used this name thereafter. St. John, the evangelist, wrote his Gospel in the city of Ephesus. Mother Mary spent the last years of her life and passed away there. The seven churches of Revelation are also located in Anatolia.

The early ecumenical councils were held in the major cities of Asia Minor; Nicaea (Iznik), Ephesos, Constantinople (Istanbul) and Chalchedon (Kadıköy).

In the first half of the 4thcen. AD., Constantine the Great altered the administrative capital of the Eastern province. The former Byzantium, renamed as Constantinople (the city of Constantine), became the capital of a huge empire and the center of a great civilization, as Christianity was recognized as the state religion. Constantinople and many other Anatolian cities were restored and adorned with outstanding monuments. The diverse history of the Empire has always been an interesting research topic by itself.

Under the Byzantine rule, Anatolia was the scene of continuous wars and eleven crusades. The Empire succeeded in driving back the Arab attacks in the

Sivas, Twin Minarets Medrese, Selçuk Period.

Konya, Medresse with narrow minaret.

7th cen. and the Pecheneks in the 11th, but could not resist the Latin invasion of the 13th cen.. The defeat of Emperor Romanus Diogenes by the Seldjuk Turks in the battle of Manzikert (1071) marks the beginning of decline that lasted till the conquest of Constantinople in 1453; thus, the end of the Byzantine Empire.

SELDJUKS, OTTOMANS AND THE TURKISH REPUBLIC: Through the years of severe drought, that ruined their homeland, Central Asia, several nomadic Turkic tribes and clans came in waves from the east, in the search for a new land to settle down. The vast fertile lands of Anatolia witnessed a most fascinating cultural synthesis in the history of mankind as they integrated with the locals and adopted their culture. They created the two great empires of Asia Minor; The Seldjuk Empire was sovereign from the second half of the 11thcen. till the invasion of the Mongolian armies (late 13th cen.); The Ottomans founded a huge world empire, that ruled from

Istanbul, Fatih Mosque and Complex.

14thcen. till the end of the 19th. They both adorned Anatolia with astounding works of art and architecture.

Anatolian Seldjuks founded the earliest Turkish state that ruled in Asia Minor. With a tolerant approach, they never interfered with the religious beliefs of the natives. Furthermore, they provided the internal peace and created a sophisticated social structure, far beyond their time, as they gave an end to the strict feudal sanctions and civil disputes. The Ottomans, with the same approach, had their own contribution to the inner peace and brotherhood; it is for this reason, the unique mosaic of diverse cultures could last for centuries.

Anatolia has always been a cross roads of the major trade routes, even before the arrival of the Turks; such as the Silk Road, Marco Polo's route, etc.. With the decline of the Byzantine Empire, the increasing anarchy and the unstable administration gave way to a stagnation in the commercial activities on the trade

Istanbul, Tophane, Kılıç Ali Mosque and Tophane Fountain, 19th century Engraving.

Mustafa Kemal Atatürk, Founder of the Modern Turkish Republic.

Sultan Süleyman the Magnificient accepts the visit of Admiral Hayrettin Barbaros (Barbarrosa).

routes. In order to reestablish commerce, the Seldjuk Turks built several Caravanserais throughout the Asia Minor and provided all that was essential. The Ottomans created a unique architectural style, as the traditional nomad life style was replaced by urban societies. The Ottoman architecture can be observed at its zenith in numerous mosques, baths, madrasahs, libraries, bridges, etc., in Istanbul and many other Anatolian cities .

The Ottoman Empire collapsed at the end of the World War I. and replaced by the young Turkish Republic, in 1923, after a legendary war for independence. As the only democratic and secular state among the Islamic countries, Turkey, with a very stable foreign policy and a fast growing economy since 1923, became part of the western world. This is clearly stated by the Customs Union Treaty with the European Council.

MARMARA REGION

The area around the Bosphorus and the Dardanelles, and the land that
surrounds the Sea of Marmara. This densely populated region stands as
the most developed area in Turkey.
Marmara, still with an important strategic location, has always been the scene
for many incidents throughout the history. Various civilizations left their
permanent traces as they passed by and several sites and cites are still the proud
owners of the masterpieces they left behind.

Istanbul, A night view of the Golden Horn from the minaret of the Süleymaniye Mosque.

ISTANBUL

Istanbul; one of the most elegant cities, not only in Turkey but in the whole world; the only city on earth that embraces the two continents, Asia and Europe; the capital city of the two great empires for almost two thousand years. Istanbul, a city that reflects the diversity of cultures, a heritage, that makes the world all the more attractive.

Considered as a leading metropolis in the world, for culture, arts, history, trade and business, Istanbul first appears on the scene of the history toward the end of the second millennium BC., as a fishing community and town called Lygos. In the 7th cen. BC., led by Byzas, a group of sailors from the land of Megare of the Aegean, came in and renamed the city as Byzantium, after their

Sunset on the Marmara Sea.

leader. Istanbul shows a fast development, as a result of its strategic location for the control of the commercial and military activities between the Mediterranean and the Black Sea and benefits from its natural harbor, Haliç, the Golden Horn. Istanbul, throughout the centuries, was the center of attraction for several states and empires, sovereign over the land of Anatolia. In the first half of the 4th.cen.BC, Istanbul was blessed as the capital of the eastern province by the Roman emperor Constantine the Great and the name was changed into Constantinople (city of Constantine).

Christianity became the official religion of the state and the empire got the earlier name of the city, Byzantium. Following the collapse of the West Roman Empire, in the dark ages of the European continent, the Byzantium remained as the only center for

23

A view of the Golden Horn from the minaret of the Süleymaniye Mosque.

knowledge and learning. The succeeding emperors decorated the city with unrivaled works of art and architecture.

With the decline of the Byzantine Empire from the 11th. cen. on, Anatolia witnessed the rise of a new civilization; the Turks. All the way from Central Asia to the vast lands of Anatolia, they attained a high level of civilization and founded several states, as they were after the great ideal to establish a world empire.

As the Ottomans extended their sovereignty to the Balkan Peninsula and forced the Byzantines to withdraw, Constantinople stood as the only stronghold of the Byzantine Empire. In 1453, Ottomans captured the city and renamed it as Istanbul and gave an end to the Byzantine rule.

Till the very last years of the Ottoman Empire, the Sultans spent tremendous efforts to preserve the architectural style and the cosmopolitan structure of the

The Blue Mosque (Sultanahmet Camii).

city. Istanbul displays the beautiful monuments of the Roman and Byzantine times next to the very best works of the Turkish-Islamic age.

Istanbul, just like Paris, Rome and London, is appraised as one of the largest and most interesting open-air museums of the world.

It is almost impossible to cover the attractions of the city within a few days time. For this reason we recommend that you make a careful plan depending on your time and interest.

HISTORICAL PENINSULA

The area to the east of the line that spans from Unkapanı, on the Golden Horn to Yenikapı, in the south, on the Sea of Marmara, is called the "Historical Peninsula" and correspond to the city under the reign of Constantine. The most important attractions of Istanbul are in this area.

Topkapı Palace

Topkapı, the administrative palace of the Ottoman Dynasty, that ruled on three continents for over six centuries, is definitely a must see. Open every day, except Tuesday, the museum and the artifacts displayed deserve a thorough attention. The construction started in 1470; the palace do not show an architectural uniformity in the classical sense as each reigning Sultan added new parts, or separate parts of it were rebuilt after the destruction of fires and earthquakes. The beautiful gardens of the palace, that occupied the eastern end of the peninsula in the time interval the palace was used by the dynasty, serve different purposes today.

Through the Central Gate, adorned with two defense towers on two sides, one reaches a large courtyard. On the left there is a chamber which was used as the barracks for the external guards, "Hallebardiers" (Teberliler) and where the imperial coaches are displayed. Along the same row is the Harem complex, which actually is a separate museum. On the right is the kitchen complex that houses four separate display rooms. The 16th.cen. construction is the work of the great Imperial Architect "Sinan". More than one thousand servants were employed in the complex and cooked for five thousand people everyday. In the religious celebrations, circumcision ceremonies for the heirs and so on, this number reached up to ten thousand or more. The large hall, that covers a great portion of the kitchen, displays one of the largest collections of Chinese and Far Eastern porcelain. The original kitchen utensils and Istanbul and European porcelain are displayed in the two small chambers at the end of the inner

Topkapı Palace, Babü's-Selam (royal reception) gate.

Topkapı Palace, Harem, Dining room of Sultan Ahmet III.

Topkapı Palace, Gate of White Eunuchs'

courtyard. The narrow building, used as the cellar in the past, houses the silver collection.

The Harem, residence of the Sultan's wives and concubines, consists of hundreds of rooms, many corridors, courtyards and halls. The intricate decoration of the complex reflects an oriental taste. Next to the Harem is the display of arms and armory; used by many Turkish and Islamic States. The Council is another attraction within the same complex.

Passing through a second monumental gate, known as the "Gate of Felicity", you reach the "Reception Hall" of the Sultan. This is where he accepted visitors, foreign envoys and the viziers.

In this courtyard, you can see the hall for the Sultan's costumes, the glamorous Imperial Treasury hall that comprises four major sections, the chamber of miniatures and Sultan's portraits, the gallery of Clocks and Watches and finally the

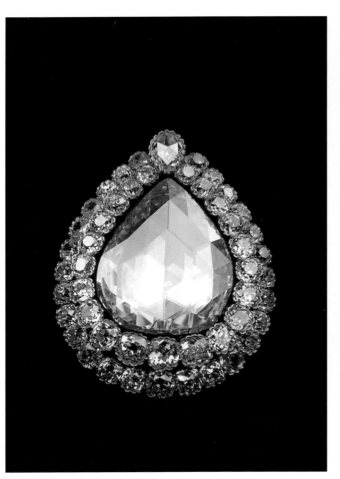

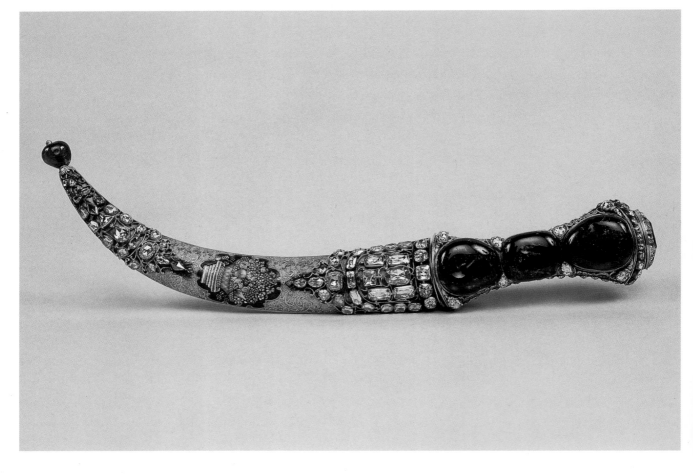

Topkapı Palace, The Treasury: Famous Kaşıkçı (Spoonmaker's) Diamond.

Enjeweled glass flask, 16th century.

Topkapı swordsman.

Topkapı Palace Baghdad Kiosk.

Topkapı Palace, Room of Sacred Islam Relics.

section of the Holy Relics. This section, especially, draws the attention of the tourists from the Moslem countries as the collection contains a letter of Prophet Mohammed, his sword and bow, flag, his mantle and his foot print. The gold cover of the black stone ("Hacer-ul Esfet"; Moslem people, during the pilgrimage, touch the stone to be relived from their sins) and a few belongings of the early Caliphs are in the same room. To the left of the Gate of Felicity is another room with a display of various fabrics and embroideries.

Three separate passes provide the access to the last courtyard. The two fine examples of civil Ottoman architecture, Revan and Baghdad Kiosks, and the special chamber for the circumcision of the heirs are located to the left of the courtyard. From the platform you can get a great view of the Golden Horn, Galata

Tower and the district and the old city of Istanbul. On the right end of the courtyard is the Mecidiye Kiosk. From the terrace in front, there is the breathtaking panorama of the city on Asia, the Bosphorus, the Sea of Marmara and the Princes Islands.

Hagia Sophia

It is a masterpiece of the Byzantine architecture and considered as the 8th. wonder of the world by most art historians. Hagia Sophia, from the 6th.cen., is the one and only construction that still stands in an excellent state of preservation and well worth an extended visit.

At first sight, you may be a little disappointed by the external view of the building;. the minarets; built in different style, the buttresses added later on and the tombs in the courtyard distort the harmony of the exterior design. However, as you enter into the basilica, used as a museum today (closed on Mondays), and get some background information on the building, it is hard not to respect and admire the people who built it and kept it in such good shape. Almost one thousand years passed before the construction of another dome that is as big as St Sophia; even today, there are only a few buildings that could be compared with St. Sophia. The two famous architects of Asia Minor, Anthemius and Isidorus, realized the dream of Emperor Justinian; a temple, bigger and more striking than the temple of Solomon in Jerusalem, with the "Wailing Wall", that still stands today. Hagia Sophia, completed in sixteen years time, was damaged several times by

Hagia Sophia Museum, mosaics. Virgin Mary, Jesus, John the Baptist.

Hagia Sophia Museum, general view of interior.

Hagia Sophia Museum, mosaics. Emperor Constantine, Jesus, Empress Zoe.

A view of the Hagia Sophia Museum from the Blue Mosque.

earthquakes and fires, but repaired, renovated and kept in use by the succeeding generations.

Hagia Sophia was converted into a mosque the day Istanbul was conquered by the Turks. Although human portrail is strictly forbidden in Islam, the mosaic and frescoes were only painted over and thus preserved, thanks to the great tolerance of the young Sultan Mehmet II.. St. Sophia became a museum in 1935 with the orders of Atatürk, founder of the modern Turkish Republic, and the decorations were brought back to daylight.

The Blue Mosque

Known as the "Mosque of Sultan Ahmet", the mosque is located next to the ancient Hippodrome and across from Hagia Sophia. The mosque was built in the first quarter of the 17th.cen.

The Blue Mosque (Sultanahmet Mosque).

The architect was Mehmet Ağa, one of the pupils of the great Architect Sinan. As he tried to surpass his master, he created a masterpiece that still has a great reputation. Next to the mosque is a religious complex, that had a soup kitchen, a hospital, a primary education school, a madrasah (school of theology) and the tomb of Sultan Ahmet.

The six minarets and the lay out of the domes and semi-domes create a unique exterior.

The decoration of the interior and the outstanding tiles are well worth seeing. A sound and light show is performed every night in various languages, just outside the mosque.

The Hippodrome

With a capacity of 100,000 spectators, the Hippodrome was the scene for the political struggles and the uprisings in the capital city of the Empire. The construction of the race tracks and the

The Blue Mosque.

The Blue Mosque, interior view. Moslem praying near the pulpit.

Hippodrome,
southern view.

Hippodrome,
obelisk.

Hippodrome
The German
Fountain.

Istanbul
Archaeological
Museum.

Istanbul
Archaeological
Museum,
Marsyas Statue.

The Cistern
Basilica
(Yerebatan
Sarayı).

cavea started in the reign of emperor Septimus Severus and were completed a hundred years later under Constantine the Great. The stones from the structure were used in the construction of the Blue Mosque. Today, the only remains from the Hippodrome are the three monumental columns and a fountain.

The granite obelisk was brought from the temple of Carnac on the river Nile, by the Roman emperor Thedosius. The second one is the "Column of the Serpent", brought from the Temple of Apollo in Delphi and the last one is the "Column of Constantine". The fountain is a present from German Kaiser Wilhelm II. to the Ottoman dynasty.

Yerebatan Sarayı
(The Cistern Basilica)

The great Byzantine cistern, located across from Hagia Sophia, was used to

supply the necessary water to the city during the barbarian attacks and when the city was under siege. 336 columns, with Doric and Corinthian capitals, were brought from various locations in Asia Minor for the construction of the cistern. A monumental aqueduct, built by emperor Valens and still a major attraction of the city, provided water to the cistern.

Süleymaniye Mosque

The mosque of Süleyman the Magnificient, located in the center of a large religious complex (külliye), stands as the most important work of Architect Sinan, one of the greatest architects in the world history. Built in the mid 16th cen., in the reign of Sultan Süleyman the Magnificient, the mosque represents the summit of the Ottoman Empire.

The monumental tombs of the sultan

and his wife, Hurrem Sultan (Roxelane) are in the graveyard to the south-east of the mosque. Among other religious constructions in Istanbul, the Suleymaniye Mosque clearly stands out as a unique example of classical Ottoman architecture with perfectly integrated sections, beautiful stained-glass windows and the extraordinary harmony of the structural elements.

Kariye Museum

This small Byzantine church (St. Savior in Chora) in Edirnekapı district, by the Theodosian wall, had been converted into a mosque and the frescoes and mosaic panels had been covered with whitewash as in St. Sophia.

In the early years of the republic, as the mosque was converted into a museum and the plaster and whitewash on the walls were cleared off, the highly

ΗΑΝΑΤΑCΙC

artistic level of the 14th cen. (Paleologs era) painting was exposed to daylight. The late 19th and early 20th.cen. wooden homes in the district, restored by the Turing Automobile Association, create an authentic ambiance that gives you the feeling of the old city

We recommend that you also see the nearby Mihrimah Mosque, which is a great work of Architect Sinan, on your visit to the Chora Museum.

The Bosphorus and The Dolmabahçe Palace

The Bosphorus, probably the most attractive and interesting strait in the whole world, still retains its beauty, even under the threat of a destructive urbanization. Istanbul is well worth a visit just for the unsurpassed beauty of the Bosphorus.

The Bosphorus is a water pass, that spans 36 km. between the Black Sea and the Sea of Marmara and 700 m. wide at the narrowest point. At this location, on either side of the strait, stands the two medieval castles built by the Ottoman Turks for the conquest of the city; the small but pretty Anadoluhisarı (14th cen.) in Asia, and right across, the awesome Rumelihisari, constructed in the 15th cen. Again on both sides of the Bosphorus, you can see the splendid homes, villas, summer palaces, woods, kiosks and gardens of Istanbul.

You can take the public ferry for a marvelous cruise on the Bosphorus, but for the visitors on an extended budget, we recommend a tour on a private boat, for a far better view.

Located along the Bosphorus, among the several palaces, that once belonged to the Ottoman dynasty, the Çırağan, Beylerbeyi and Dolmabahce stand out as

Frescoes in the Chora Church. The expulsion of Adam and Eve from Paradise.

The Bosphorus Strait, Bridge of Sultan Mehmet the Conqueror.

The Bosphorus, Rumelihisarı (Asian side fortress).

the most impressive.

The Çırağan Palace, today, is part of a five star hotel complex, whereas the other two are national museums. Beylerbeyi, without a doubt, is a beautiful palace and museum, but Dolmabahce, that reflect the splendor of the late Ottoman architecture, is a monument of wealth, decorated with beautiful Hereke carpets, chandeliers of European crystal and a rich collection of paintings. A must see.

The Islands

The isles to the south of the city are known as the "Princes Islands", as they were occupied by the exiled prices and nobles of the dynasty in the Byzantine times. Four of these islands are still occupied by the citizens of Istanbul and considered among the wealthiest districts in the city. The beautiful villas and highly decorated wooden houses, mostly used as summer homes, reflect this wealth. By the way, no motorized vehicles are allowed on the islands. There is a regular ferry service to the islands from Eminönü, by the Galata Bridge. The ferry stops at Kınalı, Heybeli, Burgaz and Büyükada successively, so you can get off the ferry in Büyükada, take a short donkey ride to Manastır Hill, enjoy the food in a local fish restaurant and catch the last ferry back to the city.

Other Places Worth Visiting

We may suggest a few other districts, sites and museums that are certainly worth seeing, for the visitors, extending their stay in Istanbul;

Archeological Museum and Çinili Kiosk in the exterior courtyard of the Topkapı Palace; The Museum of Turkish and Islamic Arts, located in the Palace of

View of the Bosphorus Strait from Dolmabahçe. Dolmabahçe Mosque. Dolmabahçe Palace and Clock Tower.

Dolmabahçe Palace, view from the air.

The islands, typical view of the Grand Island (Büyükada).

Ibrahim Pasha, next to the Hippodrome; the Carpet and Kilim Museum, by Hagia Sophia; Şehzade and Rüstem Pasha Mosques, built by Architect Sinan; Fatih Mosque, the first Ottoman religious complex in Istanbul; Yedikule and the well preserved Walls of the city, built in the reign of Theodosius; Eminönü Square, The New Mosque (Yeni Cami) and the Spice Bazaar, right next to it; Beyazıt Square and environs; The Grand Bazaar; Eyüp district on the Golden Horn; Taksim Square and the reputed İstiklal street in the new district of the city; Galata Tower; Üsküdar Square and environs, on the Asian side...

Istanbul offers great shopping opportunities as well. We strongly recommend that visitors with limited time consult with a travel agent or ask the advises of a guide.

It will certainly be advantageous to get

Egyptian Spice Bazaar (Mısır Çarşısı).

Grand Bazaar (Kapalıçarşı).

Golden Horn Bridge and Galata district.

Eyüp, the Golden Horn from the Pierre Loti Cafe.

information from and listen to the suggestions of an official guide, certified by the Ministry of Tourism. We also suggest that you keep away from the people that approach you with a broken (sometimes perfect) accent and offer you help for anything.

Ortaköy Mosque with Bosphorus Bridge in background.

43

MİMAR KOCA SİNAN
1490—1588

E D I R N E

Edirne, the former capital of the Ottoman Empire before the conquest of Istanbul in 1453, is situated on the intersection of the borders of Turkey, Greece and Bulgaria; therefore visitors, coming by land from either Greece or Bulgaria, enter Turkey through Edirne. As you approach the city from any direction, you see the four minarets of a beautiful mosque, standing on top of the only hill in the city; Selimiye.

It is worth visiting Edirne just to see this mosque which is a most attractive construction of the Ottoman architecture.

Selimiye

Considered as "the masterpiece" of the great Architect Sinan, the Selimiye Mosque (second half of the 16th.cen.) reflects the life-time achievement of the great Architect Sinan, after long years of research and the zenith of the classical Ottoman art and architecture.

In the center of a large complex, Selimiye stands out as a monument of perfection and beauty with a huge central dome , four gorgeous minarets, each with three balconies and a perfect architectural structure and uniformity.

Other Historical Places

The bazaar, located within the Selimiye complex, is the center for the commercial activities in the city and is well worth a visit.

Other places of interest; dated back to the 15, cen., Üç Şerefeli Mosque, an attractive structure reputed for the success of its plan; Muradiye Mosque, the center of a Mevlevi establishment, and the elegant Mosque of Bayezit II.

Edirne, Selimiye Mosque and monument of architect Sinan.

Edirne, Selimiye Mosque general view of interior.

Traditional Oil-wrestlers, Sarayiçi, Edirne.

B U R S A

Bursa was the capital city of the Ottoman Empire prior to Edirne. Today, it is a city of 1,5 million people and a continuously developing industrial and commercial center.

The remarkable attractions of the city will keep your interest alive all day long and you will want to stay an extra day.

Muradiye

Muradiye cemetery is the last resting place of the Ottoman Sultans and Princes, buried in their monumental tombs, in the shade of the centuries old plane trees. Next to this beautiful cemetery, the 15th cen. Mosque of Muradiye is also worth a visit.

The Mausoleum of Orhan and Osman Bey, founder of the Ottoman Empire and his son, Orhan Bey, conqueror of the city of Bursa, are located on a terrace with a spectacular view of the city and beyond.

Ulucami

Located in the commercial center of the city, next to the covered bazaar and the silk market (Kozahan), the "Grand Mosque" is one of the most attractive examples of the Ottoman architecture in the transition period. The mosque, with an interior fountain and a beautiful pulpit (a masterpiece of wood-carving), is considered a classic.

The Green Mosque

The mosque and the mausoleum, built in the reign of Sultan Mehmet I., were named as "Green", the dominant color of the interior decoration.

The grave of the Sultan is in the mausoleum, "Yeşil Türbe", adorned with attractive turquoise green tiles. Sultan Mehmet I. reestablished the Ottoman

Bursa, the Grand Mosque (Ulu Camii).

Bursa, Green Tomb.

Bursa, Green Tomb, Interior.

Bursa, Moslems praying in the Grand Mosque.

Bursa, monument to Hacivat and Karagöz (main characters of traditional Turkish shadow puppet plays).

authority after the disastrous invasion of the Mongolians (under the command of Tamerlane) in the 15th cen.; therefore he is considered to be the second founder of the Ottoman Empire. The exceptional wood work on the doors and the distinct interior decoration (especially the tiles) of Yeşil Türbe reflect the high level of expertise in the 15th cen.. Across from the mausoleum, the Green Mosque, known as the "Jewel of Bursa", stands out as a masterpiece of the early Ottoman architecture with the impressive marble work and the exquisite decoration on the facade.

Other Places of Interest

The Koza Han (Silk Market) and the Covered Bazaar that incorporates the historical Bedesten are major attractions of Bursa, worth seeing. You will change your mind after visiting the market, even if you are determined not to spend a

*İznik (Nicaea)
Museum.*

*İznik (Nicaea),
Green Mosque.*

*Bursa, Uludağ,
winter sports
center.*

*Shores of the
Apolyont Lake.*

penny in Turkey! If you have spare time, go to the famous Turkish baths in Çekirge and surrender yourself to an "expert of massage", "tellak" if a man, "natir" if a woman. As you leave, you will say, "I have never been so clean in my life!".

Yıldırım Bayezid Mosque, Emir Sultan and the Orhan Mosque are some other attraction of the city.

I Z N I K

The city is located to the east of the Sea of Marmara, by the lake that carries the same name. Iznik is a very old town with a rich cultural background and history. It became the capital of the Byzantine Empire during the 4th Crusade when Istanbul was invaded by the Latins (1204-1261).

Long before that, in 325 A.D., it was called Nicea and was the home of the famous First Ecumenical Council, making Iznik one of the main centers of Christianity.

The church of St. Sophia, well maintained city walls, the small but interesting archaeological museum and the kilns for the famous tiles are also musts on the sight-seers list.

Ç A N A K K A L E

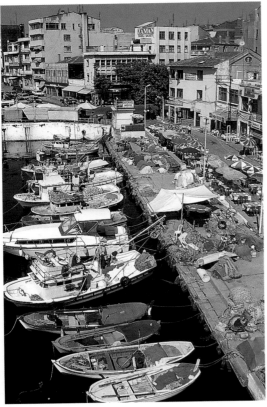

Anyone who is into the Western Culture has heard of the Dardanelles; the name of the 72 km. long strait that connect the Aegean to the Sea of Marmara. The current name is Çanakkale. Even if all the seas dry up on earth, you could still eat good fresh fish in Çanakkale. As you gaze at the waters of the Dardanelles, you get a nostalgic feel with the memories of the several leaders and personalities that crossed the strait; Persian Emperors Cyrus and Xerxes, Alexander the Great from Macedonia, Sappho of Lesbos, and of course Cleopatra and her lover Mark Anthony...

Troy is history itself

If Homer had not written the Iliad and Odyssey, Troy today would be a place of

Troy, Replica of the Wooden Horse at the entrance to the ancient city.

Town of Gelibolu (Gallipoli), center of fishing of Çanakkale (Dardenelles).

The Gelibolu National Park. English National Military Cemetary and Monument, Turkish military cemetary.

Ancient city of Troy.

interest only for archaeology fans. Other tourists would not even think of visiting there. Troy is the site of nine layers of settlement, each replacing the earlier below, and was an active city from 3,000 BC. until the birth of Jesus. Troy has been excavated many times by archaeologists such as Schliemann, Dörpfeld and many others who were searching for the treasure of Priam.

Gallipoli
"The place where a generation drowned within the water..."

The Battle of Çanakkale... In March 1915, the most powerful armed forces in history were efeated by the fierce and most clever defense of W. W. I. The peninsula today is filled with cemeteries, war museums and memories of this sanguinary war and is a chilling reminder of our recent history. If you are going to Çanakkale make sure you make a side trip to this historical site.

A S S O S

This ancient settlement dating back to the Hittite King Tutalia IV (8th century B.C.) is beautifully located off the coast of the Aegean, across the island of Lesbos. The Doric settlement, the 6th century B.C. Athena temple, the city walls and the ancient port are some of the attractions. This is a convenient stop for those traveling north to Canakkale or going south from Çanakkale.

Other Places of interest in the Marmara Region: Gemlik, on Bursa-Istanbul highway, Bursa's port of Mudanya, Kapıdağ peninsula and the Marmara archipelago (Marmara, Avşa, Pashalimanı and Ekinlik islands), Tekirdağ, the Saros bay on the Aegean Sea are other places of the region that are worth visiting.

Assos, Temple of Athena.

Assos, the Necropolis.

Assos, Temple of Athena at sunset.

Assos harbour.

AEGEAN REGION

*"The Ionians who assembled at the Panionion founded
their cities under the most beautiful sky and in
the finest climate in the known world."*

Herodotus of Halicarnassus

Bergama (Pergamum) the Acropolis, Temple of Trajan.

Ancient Theater of Priene.

P E R G A M U M

After visiting the Brandenburg Gate, a visitor to Berlin would think of visiting the Pergamum Museum. During this visit, s/he would watch the masterpiece of the Hellenistic Age the Altar of Zeus with awe. Taking advantage of the weakness of the Ottoman Empire towards the end of the 19th century, the German archaeologists carried the altar to Germany. This altar gives us an idea how beautiful Pergamum was once upon a time.

A Focus of History

Pergamum is located on the fertile plains watered by the Selinus river, therefore many civilizations have settled here since the ancient times. Having been ruled by the Lydian and Persian, Pergamum was taken over by Alexander the Great in 334 B.C. After Alexander's death, one of his generals, Lysimachus controlled Pergamum and a greater part of the Aegean region.

After Lysimachus' death, it became the center of a kingdom under Philetairos. Ruled by the kings Attalos and Eumenes, it was the governing city for all of Western Anatolia.

According to the will of King Attalus III, Pergamum became a part of the Roman Empire after his death in the second half of the 2nd century B.C.

The city experienced its golden age until the end of the 3rd century A.D. Especially after parchment was invented in this city, a library was built containing 200,000 volumes and Pergamum became a cultural center of the Roman Empire, on a par with Alexandria.

Pergamum lost its importance after the Christianity, and at one point in time it was the place of an important Jewish colony.

Acropolis

Located on top of a steep hill with a spectacular view of the surrounding area, the Acropolis (or the citadel) gives you the impression of an inaccessible fortress that could never be taken over by the enemy in the ancient times. The stone provisions for the catapults, found in the storage units as a result of the excavation, carried out by the German archeologist Carl Humann, give us an idea on the sophisticated defense systems of that time.

The sacred place Heroon is located on the left as you enter, which was dedicated to the Pergamum kings. They were believed to become gods as soon as they died. The remains of the Athena temple are reached as you walk by the city walls that show extraordinary stone working skills. The remains of the magnificent library of the ancient times are next to the temple.

Three pine trees are located in the place of the Temple of Zeus at a lower terrace. Unfortunately, today you have to go to Berlin to see the amazing beauty of "Gigantomachie" - the battle of the gods with giants on the walls of the temple!

The Temple of Trajan and its galleries can be viewed from this point that sees the Hellenistic theater.

The masonry of the vaulted substructure for the temple is outstanding. This section was used as a storage unit in the past. Above this artificial terrace is the Temenos, the sacred area of the Temple of Trajan.

Bergama (Pergamum) the Acropolis, Altar of Zeus (the altar has been removed to Berlin).

Bergama (Pergamum) the Acropolis, Theater.

As you continue towards the highest point of the Acropolis, you can see the cisterns, city walls and armory. In a complete tour of the Acropolis, you can see ruins of the kings palaces, the Temple Dionysos and the site of the foundations for the temporary stage construction of the Hellenistic Theatre.

As you go down from the Acropolis, you see the Demeter temple which has Ionian and Corinthian influences. The tour is completed with a visit to the Gymnasium and the Agora.

Asclepion

It is believed that the Asclepion (or the medical center of Pergamum) was founded by Galinus, the greatest physician of the ancient times, who is known for his great contribution to the medical science. Due to the belief, the medical center (dating back to the 4thcen) was dedicated to Asclepios, the God of health and healing.

Asclepion is reached via a sacred road, adorned with several architectural fragments from the Hellenistic Age. The ruins of the library, a well known center for scientific research, lies next to the altar area at the entrance. The Theater, used for rehabilitation, the Ionic portico, the sacred spring, latrines, the psychotherapy tunnel and the Temple of Telesphorus, used as a policlinic for consultation are located around a vast central courtyard. The Temple of Zeus Eusculape is located on the opposite side of the altar area.

The colonnaded road with a single row of shops, nearby the latrines, is also an interesting structure.

Bergama (Pergamum) Asclepion.

Bergama (Pergamum) Red Courtyard.

Kızıl Avlu (Red Courtyard)

This large temple was built using red flat bricks for the Egyptian god Serapis in the 2nd century A.D. It was converted to a church after Christianity and was dedicated to St. Paul. It is uncertain whether one of the towers of the temple was used as a synagogue by the Jews.

The Museum of Pergamum

This museum is small, but has some important collections and a visit here should complete the trip to Pergamum. It is located in the middle of the city.

While the most important artifacts were sent to Izmir, the ones of secondary importance are displayed here.

Bergama Museum, Nike Figurine.

S A R D I S

The capital of the ancient Lydia, Sardis is one of the most interesting ruins today in Turkey with its monumental buildings and location. Some of the names that people who are into archaeology and mythology know by heart are directly related to Sardis: the ancient gold river Pactolus and Croesus whose name means wealth. He minted coins for the first time in the history.

The ruins of Sardis are located at a distance of 72 km. from Izmir by the river Sard Çayı (Pactolus) close to Salihli. The earliest settlement in Sardis dates back to the second millennium BC., but the city gained importance after the 7th century B.C. when it became the capital of the Lydians. Starting with the king Giges, Sardis reached its best times during Croesus in the 6th century B.C. Croesus was enormously wealthy; he created a highly civilized society and he also had intensive relations with the neighboring states. It is known that he donated a great deal of money for the construction of the Artemis Temple, one of the Seven Wonders of the world. Croesus was defeated in the middle of this century by the Persians, the Persian king Cyrus took the treasure back to his country.

Sardis was also the end of the famous King Road that connected Persia to the western territories of Asia Minor. Sardis was then one of the three governing cities in the region. As Alexander arrived in Anatolia In the 4th century B.C., Sardis changed hands from Seleucids to Pergamum Kingdom and then to the Roman Empire. Sardis was one the seven Churches of Revelation in the early years of Christianity in Asia Minor.

The Ruins

The site is divided into two sections by the highway. The colonnaded road extends to the north of the highway. The gymnasium complex and the Synagogue,

Sardis, Temple of Artemis.

Sardis, Gymnasium

a remnant of the Jewish settlement are right behind the shopping arcade along the road. Next to synagogue is a Roman bath, down the road there are the Hellenistic theater and the ruins of the stadium.

South of the highway, as you follow the side road, you reach the 3rd century B.C. Artemis Temple, one the most beautiful temples with its Ionian style. Next to the temple, you can see the massive stone blocks of the Altar and the Marble Tower from the 3rd cen. BC., the reign of Antiochus III..

For the visitors who have the extra time; the Sardis Necropolis, nearby the Golmarmara district on the western portion of the Salihli Plain, and the tumuli of the Lydian kings next to the necropolis are worth seeing.

Sardis view fronm the Gymnasium.

I Z M I R
S M Y R N A

Izmir is the third largest city of Turkey, with a population of almost 4 million. The city is a major port and a very important commercial center, with the International Trade Fair, held every fall. Izmir has always been an active commercial port, throughout the centuries, for the export of a large variety of agricultural products, especially the rich flavored tobacco of the region, and the world famous grapes and dried figs. The rich history and the strategic location of the city, in correlation with many other historical sites on the Aegean, makes your visit all the more interesting.

The earliest settlement in Izmir, the birthplace of Homer, dates back to the 3rd millennium BC. Lelegians, the ancestors of the Carian people, were the first to settle down in the city

Towards the end of the 2nd millennium, the Hittite domination, that lasted for centuries, came to an end with the arrival of the Ionians and the city, named as Smyrna, joined the Ionian League of the twelve city states. Izmir was also an active Church in the early years of Christianity. As a result of the fast urbanization, the ancient structure of the city was largely destroyed.

The Citadel (Kadifekale) on Mt. Pagos was built in the Hellenistic times and has a great view of the city and the bay of Izmir. It has gone under several renovations in the Byzantine and Ottoman era, and today, there is almost no traces of the original construction. The Museum of Archeology houses a great variety of artifacts, including some valuable statues of the Classical Era,

İzmir, Konak Square.

İzmir, Clock Tower in Konak Square.

İzmir, view the Agora.

Izmir Archaeological Museum, Artemis, Poseidon, Demeter Stel.

Peninsula of Çeşme, Sığacık Harbour.

View from the sea, Çeşme and Çeşme fortress.

View of the shores at Çeşme in summer.

found during the excavations, carried out in various sites around the city.

The clock tower in Konak is a symbol for the city. The Kültür Park, site of the International Trade Fair and the Hisar and Şadırvan Mosques are some other attractions of Izmir, that are worth seeing. Alsancak and Kordonboyu districts are also worth a visit.

Other sites in the region

The ancient city of Claros, the site of the magnificent temple of Apollo, Notion, with a small but charming theater and a city wall, that shows a very interesting stone masonry, Teos, the site of the Dionysus Temple, and Laryssa, one of the most beautiful cities of ancient Aeolia, are worth mentioning. The skilled masonry of the city wall and the ruins of the ancient Erytrea is certainly impressive.

Çeşme, the port town of Erytrea in the ancient times, and Phokaia, the native city of the people who founded Marseilles, are attractive resort towns on the Aegean.

E P H E S U S

The city of Ephesus is one of the most interesting and extensive ancient sites in the world, and the very center of attraction in the Aegean region. The site and the ruins are highly admired by almost all visitors, on a day excursion from the cruise liners, or spending their vacation in the region.

A successful application of the grid plan, invented by the city planner Hippodamus, is clearly seen in Ephesus.

During the last years of the Ottoman Empire, Ephesus was excavated by British archaeologists and its most valuable sculptures are exhibited in the British Museum today.

The History

The earliest settlers in the region are the Carians and Lelegians, but the city, in the real sense, was established by the Ionians, in the 9th cen. BC. During the Persian invasion (6th cen. BC.), Ephesus was under the Achemenid rule, like all other Ionian cities. The Persian dominance came to an end with the arrival of Alexander the Great.

After Alexander's death, Ephesus was ruled by one of his generals, Lysimachus and it was moved to the valley between Mt. Bülbül and Mt. Panayır, where it is located today. After the Pergamum Kingdom, Ephesus was ruled by the Romans and the city had its best times during the rule of the Roman Empire. Many emperors adorned the city with exquisite works of art and architecture. The archaic Temple of Artemis is among the seven wonders of the ancient world.

St. Paul came to Ephesus many times to spread the word on the new born religion. Ephesus witnessed the rise of

Ephesus, Curetes Street.

Ephesus, Library of Celsus.

Christianity with the foundation of the Church, as the cult of Artemis constantly faded away.

The Apostle John settled in Ephesus and wrote his book of the Bible here as he lived in the city until the end of his life. It is obvious that Mother Mary came to Ephesus together with John the Apostle, after Jesus was crucified, and spent the last days of her life here in Ephesus.

In the 3rd cen. AD., Ephesus was devastated by the Goth raiders, and never retrieved the importance, nor the splendor of the past, even though the church council in 431 AD. was held here.

The continuous silting of the harbor and the epidemic diseases caused an overall decline in the commercial activities.

THE RUINS

The city is located in the valley between Mt. Bülbül and Mt. Panayır and starts at the Magnesia gate in the east and continues west towards the ancient port. The Magnesia gate was built by Vespasianus in the 3rd century A.D. on top of the Lysimachus city walls (3rd century B.C.).

As you go past the ruins of the Magnesia gate tyou will see the lofty walls and the vaulted structure of the Varius bath.

The remains of the earthenware water pipes which are a part of the world's most advanced water distribution system are located nearby. As you continue, a large area called the Upper Agora or **State Agora** and the buildings surrounding it can be seen. The Odeon (a scaled down theater building), is located behind the stoa to the north of

Ephesus, the Odeon.

Ephesus, view of the ancient city from Pritaneion.

the State Agora, adorned with fancy columns with Corinthian and Ionic style capitals.

Odeon

Built in the 2nd cen. AD., the Odeon was the assembly hall for the administrators of the city, the senators. A capacity of 1400 seats on 23 rows tells us that it was used for other purposes as well, such as concerts. The marble seats on the top rows are gone, but the bottom rows are still intact, and the griffin feet designs by the stairs outline the beauty of the Odeon. Next to the Odeon is the Town Hall, or the Prytaneion, built in the reign of Augustus, over the earlier structure, dated back to the 3rdcen. BC. In the sacred area, dedicated to Artemis, burned the perpetual fire, that was kept alive by the priests known as Curetes.

The ruins of the halls where the high ranking officials and judges used to meet are also seen closeby. The two well preserved Artemis "Polymastros" statues, found in the excavations, are kept in the Selcuk Museum today.

Curetes Way

As you walk down the track by the Town Hall, the main sewer, that goes all the way down to the ancient harbor, is seen through the grids on the street. This main sewage used to carry all the waste water of the city to the sea. This road, that leads down to the Celsus Library, is called the Curetes Street. The priests called Curetes, believed to have come from the island of Crete, used to walk down this trail to carry wood for the sacred fire and everybody who saw them would step aside. You reach the

Domitian Square as you walk by the two statue bases, decorated with Hermes and Caduceus (the wand with serpents twined around it, symbol for medicine) reliefs. Here on the right, the remains of the **Monument of Memmius** that was built by the city for Gaius Memmius is located. Gaius Memmius was an architect who built the city's aqueducts and he is believed to be the grandson of Dictator Sulla. Across from the Memmius monument is the Domitian Square. The impressive substructure of the temple, dedicated to emperor Domitian is located at the far end of the square. The partially restored Pollio Fountain is to the left of the square.

As you continue through the Gate of Hercules (named after the reliefs on the marble pedestals), the ornate statue bases and columns on either side of the street, and the store entrances behind them give you an idea on the beauty of the street in the ancient times. Further down the Curetes Street, you see the monumental fountain, built by the Roman emperor Trajan. The Terrace Houses (wealthy district of the city) are located to the left of the street. On the right, you observe the Temple of Hadrian, the Baths of Scolastikia and the public latrines, within the same complex.

Private Houses

Terrace Houses; Several artifacts and attractive mosaic panels were unearthed as a result of the excavations carried out in the past decades. The architectural style of these houses gives us important clues on the social structure of the time.

The Scolastika Bath, dated as the 1stcen. BC., was completely renovated in the 4th century. The frigidarium with a cold water pool, tepidarium (the lukewarm bathing room), caldarium (the steam room) and the apoditerium are the four major sections of the complex, typical of a Roman bath.

Ephesus, Heracles Gate.

Ephesus, Fountain of Trajan.

Ephesus, Temple of Hadrian.

The Temple of Hadrian

Next to the bath, the Temple of Hadrian displays a great architectural style. The reliefs and the decoration on the facade of this 2nd century Corinthian temple are unique. The decorative reliefs on the inner wall of the porch depicts the legendary founder of the city, Androklos, and his works. On the side street by the temple, the well preserved Latrine (the public toilet) is certainly a most impressive instance of the communal life in Ephesus. As you walk further down the Curetes Street, you will see the monumental Byzantine fountain and the octagonal tomb next to it. The Hadrian Gate is located to the left, at the end of the street. The Stoa and the monumental gateway of the Lower Agora lie next to the impressive facade of the Celsus Library. As you turn right to the Marble Street, you see the ruins of the Brothel.

Library of Celsus, Marble Street, Lower Agora and the Theater

The Celsus Library, at the intersection of the Curetes and the Marble Streets, was one of the leading restoration projects, not only in Ephesus, but in the whole world. The outstanding structure, built in the 2nd cen. AD. by a Roman Consul in the memory of his father, was perfectly reconstructed as almost all pieces were found in the excavations.

The Lower Agora is based on a square plan, measuring over a hundred meters on each side. The monumental gate of the Agora lies next to the library. The Agora is certainly fascinating with the surrounding columns and the vaulted framework of the stores. The ancient theater, at the end of the Marble Street, is one of the largest in the world, with a seating capacity of 24,000. The style is Greco-Roman; The auditorium, that leans

Ephesus, A view from the theater, the marble avenue, the agora and Library of Celsus below.

Ephesus, Theater.

on the side of Mt. Pion and the horseshoe shaped orchestra are Greek in style, whereas the (barrel) vaulted entrances are the elements of the Roman architecture. The construction of the theater started in the 3rd cen. BC., and the final form was given towards the end of the 2nd cen. AD. During the annual festival of Ephesus, concerts are organized in the theater, where St. Paul had preached in the past and once fiercely protested by the attendees.

Arcadian Street, Artemision and Other Ruins

The Arcadian, or the Harbor Street is the largest avenue in Ephesus. Extensively renovated in the reign of Arcadius, the street is quite impressive with attractive colonnades and statue bases on either side. The ruins of the Theater Gymnasium are located to the right of the street. As you walk towards the exit, a pathway on the left leads you to the well preserved ruins of the Church of Virgin Mary. The structure was

Ephesus, Artemision.

Ephesus Museum, Statue of Artemis.

Ephesus Museum, Statue of a resting warrior.

Ephesus Museum, Statue of Dionysos.

converted into a church, dedicated to Virgin Mary, at the beginning of the 4th century as Christianity became the state religion. The church was the scene of the 3rd ecumenical Council (in 431), where the practice of the Nestorians was condemned.

As you leave the site and approach the main road, you will see the Stadium on the right, in a poor state of preservation, and the ruins of the well protected Vedius Gymnasium, next to it.

The ruins of the Temple of Artemis, one of the wonders of the ancient world, are located on the opposite side of the Selcçuk-Kuşadası highway. The temple had a very important role in the religious, social and economic life in Ephesus, for over a thousand years. Today, a messy excavation site and a lone standing column are the only remnants of the once glorious Temple of Artemis.

HOUSE OF VIRGIN MARY

We know that St. John spent the last years of his life in Ephesus and wrote his Gospel here. Jesus left his mother with John, therefore, it is believed that Mother Mary came to Ephesus and lived here until the end of her life.

The remains of a basement, found next to the sacred spring, as a result of the excavations carried out on Mt. Koressos (towards the end of the 19th cen.), and the artifacts, dated as the 1stcen. A.D. by Carbon 14 dating, give proof to the belief that Virgin Mary lived here. The local Christians used to celebrate the traditional feast at the very same spot.

Today, the small chapel here is a place of pilgrimage for the Christians

from all around the world, and deeply respected by the Moslem people.

Other Places of Interest

The 14thcen. Isa Bey Mosque in Selçuk is a fine example of the early Turkish architecture in Anatolia. The Grotto of the Seven Sleepers on Mount Pion, The Basilica of St. John and the local Museum, that houses several precious artifacts, are the major attractions in Selçuk.

Home of the Virgin Mary.

Statue of the Virgin Mary.

Selçuk, Church of St. John.

Selçuk, İsa Bey Mosque.

KUŞADASI

A resort town for the wealthy citizens of Ephesus in the ancient times, and a well-known commercial port under the Ottoman rule. Today, Kuşadası is one of the most attractive resorts on the Aegean.

The 17th cen. Öküz Mehmet Pasha Caravanserai (from the Ottoman times), is the only historical attraction in the city, in a good state of preservation.

Till the 70's, Kuşadası was a small, quiet coastal town, but today, it is under the threat of an intensive urbanization and environmental destruction, and unfortunately, the city center has lost its authenticity.

Kuşadası, Harbour.

Kuşadası, a general wiev.

Ancient city of Priene, Theater.

P R I E N E

As you travel south from Kuşadası, the National Park on the "Dilek" Peninsula is well worth a visit. You can enjoy the tempting waters of the Aegean, at the beautiful beaches of the park.

As you pass the town, Söke, you reach a large plain, irrigated by the Meander (Menderes) River. Known as the Latmos Bay in the past, the area was silted in with alluvial soil carried by the river, throughout the centuries. On a hillside to the north of the plain, there is the ruins of the ancient city of Priene, one of the most exciting sites from the archaic times.

The site displays the very best application of the grid plan (all streets intersect at right angle), put forward by the city planner, Hippodamos.

The city was entirely deserted in the second half of the 12th century, due to problems in transportation as a result of the silting and the malaria disease.

As you walk up the hill, you will be most amazed by the extraordinary masonry of the city wall.

The Hellenistic Theater and the Temple of Athena

The well preserved theater building was renovated, in great detail, in the Roman times, but still carries all the common features of a Hellenistic theater.

You reach the Temple of Athena through the ruins of the Byzantine church, next to the stage construction. The Ionion style temple is a masterwork of Pytheos, the architect of the famous Mausoleum, one of the seven wonders of the ancient world.

Further down, you can see the Sacred Portico, the Agora, and the ruins of the

houses on either side of the road, that leads to the ancient port.

On the way back, the lower pathway takes you to the Prytaneion, or the Town Hall, and the "Bouleuterion", the administrative center of the city.

The Bouleuterion, designed as a square, is in an excellent state of preservation; the pedestal deserves a particular attention. Across the street are the remains of the small Temple of Zeus, in Doric style. The remains of the Upper and the Lower Gymnasium, and the Temple of Demeter are in a poor state.

MILETUS

You depart from Priene and continue south. As you leave the plain behind, you see a splendid theater building on the left; the road leads you to Miletus, one of the most attractive sites in the region; the city, where the historian Hecataeus, Thales, and Anaximenes and Anaximander, the nature philosophers, were born and raised.

The history of Miletus dates back to mid Bronze Age (roughly 16thcen. BC), but the information, on the early phase, is quite uncertain. The Mycenaean pottery, found in the excavations, give us clues on the early settlers, the people of Crete (Strabon also confirms that). However, Homer suggests that it was the Carians, who settled in the area for the first time. Nevertheless, it is certain that

Ancient city of Priene, Temple of Athena.

Miletus became a major capital under the Ionian control, and a wealthy city, as an outcome of the ongoing trade, with the colonies in the region.

During the invasion, Miletus was razed down by the Persians, as the city had an active role in the Ionian Revolt, against the Persian rule. In the middle of the 5thcen. BC., the city was rebuilt on a well-organized plan.

Miletus had its heydays in the Roman times. The city lost its importance as a result of the silting of the harbor, during the Byzantine era, and faded away from the scene of history.

The theater building is the most significant part of the ruins, and admired by all visitors, even those, who do not have a deep interest in archeology. Built in the 2nd cen. AD., the building was kept in a good state of preservation.

The colossal theater, that has a capacity of 15,000 spectators, is a remarkable structure, with its elegant royal box and spacious galleries.

Through the theater building and the nearby Faustina bath, you continue on to the actual site. At this point, the Ilyas Bey Mosque, from the 15th century is worth mentioning. The building is an interesting example of the early Ottoman architecture, and the stonework is particularly impressive. As you tour the ancient site, you will also see the wheat silos, the monumental gate of the Agora, the Town Hall, the gymnasium complex, the harbor monument and the gate, and the sacred Delphinion, among other ruins.

The artifacts of secondary importance, found in the excavations, are displayed in the local museum, nearby the entrance to the site.

Miletos, Theater.

D I D Y M A

As you leave the city of Miletus and travel south for a short while, you will see the giant Ionian columns at a distance, over the rooftops; the columns of the astounding Temple of Apollo.

The largest "dipteros" (surrounded with a double row of columns) style temple of the ancient times; Didymaion or the Temple of Apollo. The only colossal temple, that still stands in good shape, after the destruction of the competing temples in Ephesus and Samos. An ancient temple, built over a sacred spring, and measures one hundred by fifty meters.

Didyma Temple of Apollo, frieze detail.

Didyma , Temple of Apollo.

The construction of the temple started in the Hellenistic Age, over the ruins of the archaic sanctuary of Apollo and the oracle center, dedicated to the cult, and it was never completed as Christianity became the official religion.

The Temple of Apollo is a masterpiece of the Ionian architecture. It is all the more striking with the unique reliefs on marble, and the well preserved galleries that shows almost no sign of deterioration, over the two thousand years since the time of construction.

*Didyma ,
Temple of
Apollo.*

Altınkum.

You leave Didyma and continue south; soon, you enter the Carian territory. You reach Halicarnassos, the contemporary town of Bodrum, well known for the monumental burial of the Persian Satrap Mausolus, the Mausoleum, built by the architect Pytheos. On your way to Halicarnassos, you may take your time to see the natural wonders of the region.

One other ancient settlement, Heracleia ad Latmos is also worth a visit. You will be tempted by the well preserved Hellenistic walls of the city, the Athena Temple, Agora, Town Hall, the theater, and the streets, located according to the grid plan of Hippodamus. The lake, mountain and history; a great spot for photographers!

Continue on to Euromos, an outstanding Corinthian temple, dedicated to the mighty god of the Greek pantheon, Zeus.

Many interesting artifacts have been unearthed by the Italian archeologists in ancient Iasos, on a secondary route before you arrive in Milas.

The road to the left from Milas takes you to the ancient city of Labranda, which is definitely worth seeing. Another beautiful temple for Zeus and a monumental road...

You continue on your journey watching the spectacular scenery along the road, and...

Milas, Euromos, Temple of Zeus.

Iasus Quay, fish restaurant.

Bodrum is a splendid resort town.

B O D R U M
H A L I C A R N A S S O S

It may be fortunate or not, who knows. Bodrum is not the same as it was thirty years ago, a charming, virgin coastal town. Bodrum, today, is a popular resort town, that drags millions of people every year.

Only the foundations of the Mausoleum remain today, but it is still worth seeing, as well as the over restored theater construction.

The Castle of St. Peter, or with the contemporary name, the Bodrum Castle, was built by the Knights of Rhodes. It was the last outpost of the knights, in Asia Minor, till the Ottoman occupation in the 16th century.

The castle incorporates one of the most important museums of underwater archaeology, in the world; definitely a must see.

Then you can dine in a town restaurant, and have fish and local wine, or you plan to take a boat ride, the "Blue Voyage".

The word "beautiful" fails to describe the scenery. Unspoiled bays, the incredible harmony of the clean, still waters of the Aegean and the forest, tranquillity and peace; this is the "Blue Voyage", a dream vacation, that you will never forget.

We advise you to stay a few more days in the area, and enjoy the beautiful bays and beaches on the Bodrum Peninsula.

Marmaris and the Marmaris harbour.

TOWARDS LYCIA

Further south, past the city of Muğla, you are on the way to the ancient Lycia. The southwestern corner of Turkey, known as the "Turquoise Coast", has plenty of attractions to see; many resort towns, beautiful villages and ancient sites. As you pass the ruins of Idyma, that hardly satisfies the greed of an amateur archeologist, you end up in a resort town, that reminds you of Bodrum; Marmaris.

The modern town extends over the ruins of the ancient Physeus and today, it is one of the most attractive resorts on the Turquoise Coast. It is also possible to go to Rhodes from Marmaris by boat.

Nightlight in Bodrum.

Bodrum, typical summer scene.

MARMARIS

The town offers a great deal of opportunities for the visitors, with several convenient accommodations and beautiful beaches nearby. The medieval castle in the downtown and the traditional houses of the past centuries within the walls create a picturesque setting. You may be interested in the ruins of Asartepe, 2 kilometers from the city center. The Hellenistic city walls, that are still in good shape, are worth seeing.

The ancient city of Knidos lies at the tip of the Datça peninsula. The site is reached by a secondary road or by boat. It is also possible to take a boat from Bodrum to go to Knidos.

Heading east this time, you arrive in the town Köyceğiz, a marvelous resort, on the lake known with the same name. In the last years, there is an increasing

number of foreign visitors in the town, but Köyceğiz has always been a popular spot especially for the local tourists. An isthmus, and a fishing weir, separates the less salty waters of the lake, and the sea. The lake is still very clean despite the fast urbanization around it. The people of Köyceğiz are very hospitable, and the town is ideal for a peaceful and pleasant vacation. The ancient city of Kaunos, well known for the marvelous Lycian tombs, is well worth a visit, and you reach the site by a pleasant boat ride. The rock cut tombs, well preserved theater, and the lay out of the city makes Kaunos a very attractive site.

Marmaris, the shore in front of Hisarönü.

Datça, fish here always receive special praise.

Köyceğiz, Rock-cut tombs of Dalyan.

Cnidus, a view of the harbour from the theater.

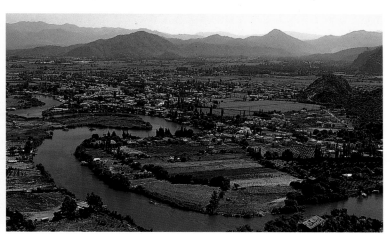

Knidos, a view of the harbour from the theater.

Köyceğiz, Dalyan general view.

Dalyan, İztuzu Beach.

FETHIYE TELMESSOS

As you travel further east along the coastline, you arrive in Fethiye, on a bay of incredible beauty surrounded by a steep mountain range.

The town Fethiye is one of the best organized vacation spots in Turkey. A boat ride is no doubt the best way to explore the bay area, and the islands off shore if you have the time for it.

Telmessos, a renowned port town of ancient Lycia (and the environs), is among the greater attractions in the area. The reputed Tomb of Amyntas, on a hillside to the east of the town, and the ruins of the Byzantine castle are certainly worth seeing.

A short way from Fethiye is the Ölüdeniz (the Dead Sea), one of the most beautiful beaches in the world.

From this point on, you will be visiting the Lycian cities. But first, let us hit the road to see the two fascinating sites in the north; Aphrodisias and Pamukkale, or with the ancient name, Hierapolis.

As a matter of fact, you can easily get to Aphrodisias or Pamukkale, via Ephesus. It takes approximately two, or two and a half hours by car. En route, you will have the opportunity to see the ruins of ancient Nysa, nearby the town of Sultanhisar.

The charming theater construction, the interesting water canals, and the well preserved Town Hall of the city are among the very best you can see.

APHRODISIAS

Aphrodisias was one of the most important settlements in ancient Caria, and a community of an amazing wealth. Today, the ancient site has some of the best preserved ruins of the antiquity, deeply admired by all visitors.

The earliest known settlement dates back to the Bronze Age (3,000 BC.). The city had its heydays in the Roman times. With the strong influence of the Mother Goddess cult in Anatolia, Aphrodite, the Goddess of Love, surpassed the cult of Zeus (just like Artemis in Ephesus), and was worshipped as the protector Goddess of the city, named after her. In the Christian era, The Byzantine State changed the name of the city into Stavropolis (city of the cross), in order to efface the influence of the Aphrodite cult, and Aphrodisias became the center of a diocese.

Dated as the 1stcen. BC., the Ionic Temple of Aphrodite was converted into a church by the Byzantines. The structure is still intact, despite the alternations through the centuries.

The monumental gate to the Temple, the Tetrapylon, is a masterwork of the Roman architecture. The well preserved, all marble theater, the unusual Agora, and the outstanding Stadium of enormous proportions are absolutely worth a visit.

The artifacts of greater importance from the excavations are on display in the small museum, at the entrance of the site. A visit to this museum should complete the tour in Aphrodisias. However, hundreds of important findings are kept in the courtyard outside the museum, due to limited space, or simply the abundance of the new findings.

Aphrodisias, Tetrapylon.

Aphodisias, Temple of Aphrodite.

Aphrodisias, Theater.

Aphrodisias, The best-preserved stadium in Anatolia.

PAMUKKALE HIERAPOLIS

The site is located a half hour drive from Denizli, the provincial capital. The ancient city of Hierapolis is part of the (natural) setting, originally known as Pamukkale.

The ancient site has been severely damaged as a result of the recurrent earthquakes, and unfortunately, only a few structures remain standing. The ancient site is most famous with the impressive "Necropolis" (the cemetery) of incredible size. The extremely well preserved Theater with perfect marble reliefs, and the monumental gate with round towers on either side, built in the honor of emperor Hadrian, and the colonnaded road behind it are a few of the attractions in the site. The Roman Bath, that was converted into a church in the Byzantine times, and the tomb (Martyrium) of St. Philip, built over a complicated plan, are also interesting places to see. The renovated Roman bath, nearby the Theater, is used as a local museum today. The healing power of the thermal springs in the area was the reason why thousands of people in the past came to Hierapolis for a cure. Those who were cured went back to their homeland, but others that died here were buried in the extensive cemetery of the city, in their own burial customs. Therefore the Necropolis has a variety of burials and distinct tombs; tumuli, Lycian sarcophagi (like an overturned boat), house type tombs, etc.

The astounding natural site attracts people from all around the world, and the formations look almost unreal. The rich calcium content of the mineral water from the nearby thermal springs is the major cause behind the amazing land formations. In other words, the lime residue, after the carbon gas evaporates,

Hierapolis, swimmers in the antique pool.

Hierapolis, Frontinus Gate.

Pamukkale Museum, Marble Sarcophagus.

Pamukkale Travertines.

A general view of a natural wonder, the Pamukkale Travertines.

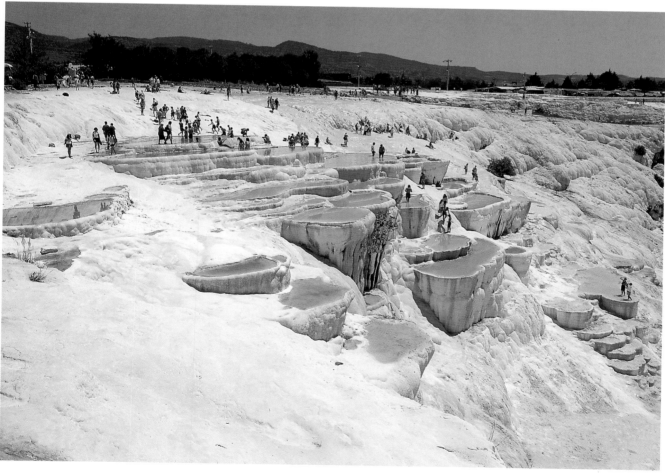

Xanthus Theater.

create the visual miracle; the travertines, and the pools on top of each other. You can walk on the travertine terraces, but only barefoot, and put your feet in the lukewarm mineral water.

L Y C I A

Let us go back and continue our journey east along the Mediterranean. We are now in ancient Lycia.

The region between Caria and Pamphylia is known as Lycia. The earliest remains in the region are from the 7th cen. BC.. The well preserved Roman and Hellenistic ruins, various temples and tombs, as well as a few pre Hellenistic monuments (from the 5th and 4th centuries BC.) are worth seeing in the area.

Especially the rock cut tombs represent a unique architectural style. According to Heredotos, the Lycians came from the island of Crete under their leader Sarpedon, who was mentioned in Illiad as an ally of the Trojans.

Lycians were the only people in Asia Minor that stood against the Lydian rule, but the brave people of Lycia could not resist the Persian invasion in the 6th.cen. BC.

X A N T H U S
K I N I K

The name comes from the river next to the town and it means yellow in Greek language. According to Heredotos, the town was independent until the Persian invasion.

Xanthus, Alongside the theater, Harpies Monument.

A significant event in the history of Xanthos was the war against the Persian commander Harpagos. The people of Xanthos realized that they were going to lose the battle, so they went back and burned their city including all the women and children in 545 BC.

The families that survived this mass suicide rebuilt the town together with other immigrants.

In the 5thcen. BC., a great fire destroyed the city. In 42 BC, Xanthos was devastated this time by Brutus, and was rebuilt a year later by Marcus Antonius.

Xanthos is well known for the monumental tombs. The Harpy monument is almost 9 meters high and the actual burial section is decorated with reliefs that depicts a king and his wife accepting gifts from their children and other members of the family.

The tomb is dated as the 5thcen. BC., based on the style of the reliefs. To the north of the Agora, the tall stele has inscriptions in Lycian language on all four sides, and a Greek poem that consist of twelve verses. The Lycian pillar tomb is shaped like a sharp edged sarcophagus. According to the Lycian faith, the lid of the tomb shaped as an overturned boat, is defined as follows; "Life is like a boat flowing down the river, and with the death, the boat sinks".

Xanthos is one of the most interesting and attractive sites on the Mediterranean coast.

LETOON

Located only four kilometers away from Xanthos, Letoon was the sacred city in the Lycian union. The name comes from Leto, Apollo and Artemis" mother. Three important temples are located here, as well as a beautiful monumental fountain, the ruins of a Byzantine monastery and an ancient theater that is still not excavated.

PATARA

Patara was the most important port town in Lycia, and the judicial center for the Roman governor at the time. St. Nicholas (Santa Claus) was born and raised in Patara. According to a few sources, the town was an oracle center of Apollo, active only in the wintertime.

(You should take a swim if you have the time)

Letoon, Detail of the architectural elements of the Temple of Artemis.

Patara, Monumental gate to the birthplace city of St. Nicholas.

KAŞ
ANTIPHELLOS

The ancient Antiphellos is located a kilometer to the west of the charming vacation spot, Kaş. The Hellenistic style theater, with 26 rows, is in an excellent state today.

The city walls were built on steep rocks and reached a height of 7 meters. On the north eastern hillside, you can see the rock cut tombs and burial monuments, decorated with inscriptions in the Lycian language.

Kaş Lycian sarcophogus in the town proper.

Kaş, a very pleasant vacation spot.

Kalkan.

K E K O V A

A spectacular view of Kekova from the castle at Simena.

A view of Simena (Kaleköy) from the Sea.

Kekova, Manastır Bay.

Kekova, Üçağız Village and Lycian sarcophagi.

Kekova, a Lycian sarcophogus emerging from the sea.

Kekova is certainly one of the most interesting spots along the Turkish Mediterranean coast. The mystery of the region lies in its geography. The tectonic activity taking place in the Taurus Mountains caused the Kekova peninsula to sink and thus the city of Simena slipped under the waters of the Mediterranean.

Three kilometers up the road, in the town of Kale (near the ancient sites of Demre and Myra), the visitor can hire a motorboat and get a tour that lasts four hours or so. The tour takes the visitor around the peninsula and here one looks down into the water at the ancient city and its walls, the drainage system, the bath, the staircases and other ruins. The ancient harbor lies a few meters beneath the surface of the water.

On the way back, the boat leaves the Kekova coast and goes towards a village on the mainland. As the town was built just beyond the historical castle it is called "Kaleköy" (Fortress Village). As you get near the village, you will get the impressive view of the modest fishermen cottages and the outstanding Lycian sarcophagi, especially the one to the left that lies submerged in the shallow waters of the bay. These tombs, especially those partially submerged, have become the symbol of the Kekova National Park.

The ancient city of Simena was founded in the first century BC. on the attractive peninsula, and was an important trade center of the time. The extensive harbor of the city was well protected at all times, even when the storms were raging on the Mediterranean. As a result, Simena became a favored anchoring spot for the sailors.

MYRA
KALE-DEMRE

The ancient Myra was one of the six largest cities in Lycia, and a capital city for a while. The city was given the right to mint coins in the 3rd and 2nd centuries BC. St. Nicholas, also known as Santa Claus lived in Myra as a priest and St. Paul stopped here on his trip to Rome and met with other disciples, making Myra a religiously significant place in history.

The rock cut tombs in Myra are some of the best preserved in the region. The Roman theater is also in a perfect condition.

Demre (Kale), St. Nicholas Church, statue of St. Nicholas.

Two interior views of the Church of St. Nicholas.

Lycian rock-cut tombs at the necropolis, southern end of the ancient city, Myra.

O L Y M P O S
Ç I R A L I - Y A N A R T A Ş

Located at the opening and on both sides of a river, Olympos was founded in the 3rd century BC. A member of the Lycian federation, the city was under the invasion of the Cilician pirates until 78 B.C. and then became a part of the Roman empire. Today, the most interesting structure here is the remains of the portal of a temple, located to the west of the river.

In Chimera near Olympos, a flame comes out of the ground constantly. The people of Olympos built a temple here by the perpetual flame for their mighty God Hephaistos (or Vulcain in the Roman mythology, and Hittite in origin). As you can see in the Anatolian Civilizations Museum in Ankara, the God is portrayed as a fire breathing, goat headed lion with

Olympos, beach at Çıralı.

The "burning stone".

*Phaselis,
View of the
peninsula.*

*Phaselis, the
Roman Bath.*

the wings of an eagle and the tail has a snake head.

P H A S E L I S

Located in the midst of a wonderful natural setting, the city was founded by the Rhodesians in the 6th century B.C. The city had three separate ports; north, middle and south ports. You can see the remains of the Roman baths and the gate of Hadrian, as well as the Agora and the theater complex, on either side of the large avenue that once connected the north and south ports. At the opening of the middle port, the remains of the wall to stop the waves from entering the port are seen. The partially intact aqueducts are worth seeing. You may go all the way up the ancient theater, overlooking all three ports and enjoy the scenery.

Antalya, harbor in the ancient citadel.

Kemer, an arial view of the most modern harbour along the Mediterranean.

Kemer, Park and beach in the monlight.

ANTALYA

The city of Antalya is one of the most important tourist centers in Turkey.

During the excavations, artifacts dating far back to the Paleolithic Age were found in the Karain cave to the northwest of the town. The area was ruled by the Hittites between 1900 and 1200 BC. The independent city states of Pamphilia, Lycia and Cilicia were sovereign till the Phrygians. Dominated by the Lydians for a while, the province was invaded by the Persians in the 6thcen. BC.

The Persian domination came to an end with the arrival of Alexander the Great, and after his death, his generals ruled the area. Antalya, named after the Pergamum King Attalos II. (founder of the city), became a district of the Roman Empire in 67 BC. The city was conquered by the Seldjuk Turks in 1085. After a short interval of Byzantine rule, Antalya became an Ottoman province in 1426. Between 1919 and 1921, the city was under Italian occupation.

During the crusades, the knights set sail from Antalya on their way to Palestine. As the new city of Antalya extends over the ancient site, there is not much left of the ancient Attaleia. The Kocaali Park, Yivli Minare, Hadrian's Gate and the outstanding Museum of Archeology as well as Kaleiçi (Old Town), or the inner citadel are the greater attractions in the town.

YIVLI MINARE (FLUTED MINARET)

A fine example of the Seldjuk architecture, Yivli Minare is the symbol of Antalya. The brick minaret sits on a square base and is decorated with mosaic shaped blue stones and tiles. The 45

meter high minaret was built as an additional part of the structure next to it, an old Byzantine church that was converted into a mosque by the Seldjuk Sultan Alaeddin Keykubat. The Sedjuk mosque seen today was built in the 14thcentury over the ruins of the church.

THE MUSEUM OF ARCHEOLOGY

One of the best museums in Turkey; several Prehistoric objects, and a large variety Hellenistic, Roman and Byzantine artifacts (as well as Seldjuk and Ottoman relics) are on display in the chronological order.

Antalya, Yivli Minare, the symbol of the city.

Antalya, view of the citadel from the marina.

Antalya, Hadrian's Gate.

Antalya, Archaeological Museum.

Antalya, Düden waterfalls.

TERMESSOS
Güllük Dağı

Termessos is located on a 1050 meter high plain between two mountains, about 30 km north-west of Antalya. Termessos is the only city which Alexander could not conquer. The city had its best times during Hellenistic ages and under Roman rule. During the Roman rule, the people of Termessos were given the right to write their own law. After this bright period, the city was totally vacated in the 5th century. The people of Termessos describe themselves as Solymi, af the Mt. Solymus, the Modern Güllük Dağ, a local group from Pamphylia.

The entrances to the city are from the north and south in the valley. After the entrance, the roads go south-west, then south towards necropolis and connect around gymnasium. There are paths which connect the gymnasium to the theater from the Odeum direction and the buildings to the stoa. On the side of these paths which were mostly built in the 2nd century, the drainage system can be seen.

Seven temples were found south of the city. The Zeus Solymeus temple is about 4 meters high. The well preserved Artemis temple has inscriptions at the door saying that the temple was built by a woman named Aurelia Almasta with her own money and the cult sculpture was built with help from her husband. The Corinthian temple which was built during the late Roman era, the Main Temple built by the Antoninus (2nd century A.D.) and the Templum in Antis also can be visited. Besides the temples, there is a Hellenistic theater with a capacity of 4,200 people, water and olive oil cisterns carved in rocks and the Bouleterion. Bouleterion is the best preserved building in Termessos and considered to be a masterpiece in stonework.

Termessos, Theater.

Termessos, the Necropolis.

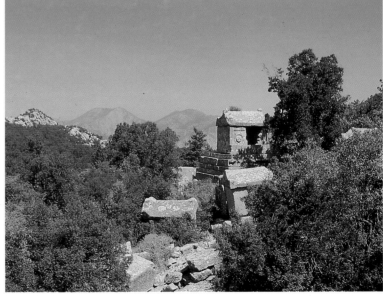

P E R G E
A K S U

According to the ancient sources and legends, the city was founded by Greek heroes after the Trojan War. A Hittite tablet found in Hattusa gives the name of the city as Parha. The coins found in the excavations depict the cult statue of the local goddess Artemis Pergaia.

The earliest settlers in the area were the Acheans (roughly 2000 BC.). In the 7thcen. BC., the city was occupied by the Greeks that came from the Aegean islands and the western provinces of Asia Minor. The Lydian rule in the 6thcen. BC. came to an end by the Persian invasion. The city was conquered by Alexander the Great in 333 BC. After his death, the Seleucid dynasty and later, the Pergamum Kingdom ruled the area. The 2ndcen. BC. was the beginning of the Roman mastery that lasted for centuries. The people of Perge accepted Christianity in the 4th century. The Seldjuk Turks gave an end to the Byzantine rule in the region, and in the 15th century the Ottoman Empire was sovereign.

The city developed in two major parts; the acropolis and the lower city. The city initially occupied the fifty meters high Acropolis area and as time passed enlarged down towards the lower plain. The lower city was reorganized according to the grid plan put forward by Hippodamos.

The ancient theater had a seating capacity of 15000. The two stories of the stage construction, and the proscenium in particular, are in excellent state of preservation. The reliefs on the stage building depict the life story of Dionisos, the God of Wine; born premature, he is placed in Zeus' body, then the messenger God Hermes leaves the child to the care of the nymphs. Another relief portrays

Perge, the Theater.

Perge, the gate of the Hellenistic city.

Colonaded Street, Perge.

the god seated on a regal chariot pulled by panthers in the company of the Satyrs.

The well preserved stadium could seat 12000 people. The barrel vaulted sections along the supporting structure (for the auditorium) served other purposes as well. Majority of these rooms were used as shops, and the audience entered the stadium by the doors, through the substructure.

The city had three main entrances. The Hellenistic Gate, located behind the Roman gateway at the entrance to the site, has an oval shaped courtyard. As you pass through this gate, next to the courtyard are the remains of the two tiered gateway (with arched entryways) built by Plancia Magna, a woman recurrently mentioned in the inscriptions. The main street of the city, commercial Agora, Roman bath and the monumental fountain next to it are also worth seeing.

Perge, Gate of the Hellenistic city.

Perge, Frieze on the Theater.

Aspendos, monumental theater.

ASPENDOS

The city of Aspendos is located on the ancient Eurymedon. Established by the colonists from Argos, the city is known all over the world for the attractive Roman Theater, that is still in excellent shape. In the 5th cen. BC., Side and Aspendos were the only cities that were given the right to mint silver coins. The city walls were built in the Hellenistic Age and underwent extensive renovations in the Roman and Byzantine times.

The ancient city should be observed in two major parts; the Acropolis (upper city) and the Lower City. The Agora, Bouleterion, Basilica and the monumental fountain in the upper part of the town, and the Theater building, Stadium, Roman Bath and the Aquaduct in the lower section are certainly worth seeing.

Aspendos Theater: With a seating capacity of 15000, the Theater was built by the famous architect Zenon in the reign of emperor Marcus Aurelius (second half of the 2ndcen. AD.). It is the best preserved theater building of the ancient times. As in the Hellenistic approach, a small section of the auditorium leans on the hillside by the Acropolis. The rest of the building stands over a vaulted substructure.

The tall stage building isolated the audience from the rest of the world. The very top section of the structure was partially renovated, and the acoustics were enhanced with later additions. The stage building was used as a caravanserai in the Seldjuk times, and the structure was constantly renovated and maintained in good shape. As a result, the theater has survived to our day without losing none of the vital features.

S I D E

According to Strabon, Side was founded by the settlers from Cyme, an Aeolian city to the north of Izmir. The word "Side" meant pomegranate in the local dialect. According to the findings in the recent excavations, Side was under the rule of the Ptolemai dynasty of Egypt in the 3rd cen. BC. After an interval of Syrian dominance, the city gained independence in 188 BC. A hundred years later, in 78 BC., Side was annexed by the Galatians. The city was the scene for the Arab attacks and piracy in the following centuries, and after the 3rd cen. AD., Side was no longer an active commercial port.

After you pass through the gate of the city, you arrive at a large area decorated with flat stones. This is the beginning of the two main streets. On either side of the streets are the decorative porticos and remains of the shops behind them. The column capitals are Corinthian style. Across from the gate, you can see the huge monumental fountain, the "Nymphaion".

The square shaped Agora is surrounded by colonnaded galleries, and the shops were located on the three sides. In the center of this area are the remains of an altar dedicated to the city Goddess Tyche, the Queen of Fortune.

The Theater next to the Agora is quite impressive, and has a great view of the whole city.

From here, you can see the remains of the ancient harbor, the temples, and the monumental road invaded by the contemporary town.

Side, the Beach.

Side, the Agora and Museum.

View of Side and the Side Theater from the air.

Side, Temple of Apollo.

Side Museum, Statue of Heracles.

Side Museum, Marble statue of Hermes.

114

Alanya, Harbour.

Alanya, view of the citadel from one of the beaches.

A L A N Y A

The ancient name of the city is "Korakesion". Alanya is known for the outstanding castle and shipyard, built by the great Seldjuk Sultan Alaeddin Keykubat.

The Red Tower (Kızıl Kule), named after the red stones and bricks used in the construction, was also built in the reign of Sultan Keykubat.

The huge tower is more than 33 meters high, and consists of five stories on an octagonal base. It was built rather like a castle, and the idea was to protect the harbor of the city.

The Alara Fortress and the Summer Palace (Hamamlı Kasr) are the other attractions in Alanya worth seeing.

The frescoes used in the decoration of the dome in the bath (within the palace complex) are particularly impressive.

View of Alanya from the Citadel: Red Tower and Harbour.

The Damlatas cave by the town that has stalactites and stalagmites formed in 15 million years time, is also worth seeing.

Alanya, Alara Creek and Alara Citadel.

Alanya, Cleopatra's Beach.

Alanya Citadel.

Alanya has an active night life during the summer months.

p. 120-121: Two antique bridges and the canyon over the Köprü Creek.

Manavgat, the Waterfalls.

Kızkalesi (fortress) located between Mersin and Silifke.

Anamur, Mamuriye Fortress.

S I L I F K E

Silifke, the center of the ancient Cilicia, was established by Seleukos, one of the generals of Alexander the Great in the 3rd century BC. The famous fortress, built in the 7th century, is worth seeing even today with the towers, cellar and the cistern. Also the bridge over the Göksu river with its six arches near the city is worth seeing.

An inscription on the bridge says that the structure was built by Emperor Vespasianus and his sons Titus and Domitianus. The German Emperor Friedrich Barbarossa, who commanded the third Crusade, drowned as he was trying to cross the river.

The Aya Tekla church in Silifke also has special importance in the history of Christianity. It was built in 337 AD by the

Uzuncaburç, Temple of Zeus.

Roman Emperor, Constantine the Great, who was also the founder of the Byzantine Empire, and was dedicated to Saint Thekla, one of Saint Paul's disciples.

A N A M U R

The Assyrian dominance (roughly 800 BC.) came to an end with the Persian invasion. After the Persians, the city of Anamur was ruled by the Macedonian Empire and the Seleucid dynasty. It was later given to Commagene King Antiochos, by Emperor Caligula during the Roman rule beginning in the first century BC. It later changed hands many times between the Byzantines and the Arabs. It was ruled by the Seljuks in the 9th century, and later by the Karamanoğlu Principality and the Ottomans. Zigzag shaped city walls were uncovered in the excavation. In the

Silifke, Rock-cut reliefs.

Upper City there is a theater, an odeon, a Roman bath with interesting mosaics, a basilica and a street leading to the lower city. The Necropolis is in the Lower City. The fortress, built by the Romans in the 3rd cen. AD., was extensively renovated, and altered by the Seldjuk Turks as a mosque, fountain and a bath were added to the complex.

UZUNCABURÇ

Situated 30 kilometers north of Silifke, Uzuncaburç was built over the ruins of the ancient city of Olba, known with the name Diocesarea in the reign of Emperor Vespasianus. The ancient theater from the 2nd cen. AD., a monumental gate built in the Roman era, and the Temple of Zeus, built in the Corinthian style in the 3rd cen. AD., are the important attractions in the town, that are worth seeing.

CORYCUS
Heaven - Hell

There are two large caves at the site, situated 50 km north of Mersin. The natural caves, formed as a result of earthquakes and land erosion are called "Heaven and Hell." At the entrance of the cave, named as Cennet (heaven) regarding the beautiful trees and grasses, are the ruins of a church from the 7th century.

The other cave has a truly frightening look and is named Hell. There are local sayings that the sinners and criminals were thrown in here in the ancient times. Very near these caves are the remains of the ancient Corycus ruins and also the remains of the fortress.

TARSUS

As you continue towards east, you get to Tarsus, the birthplace of St. Paul and

Uzuncaburç, two views of the ancient city.

Corycus, entrance to the Cave of Paradise and chapel.

his native land. There is a deep well in the place of the former house where Paul was born. The water from the well is believed to have healing powers. According to the famous geographer Strabon, the city was founded by the people of Argos, in search of Io, Zeus" wife. The city was ruled by the Hittites, Assyrians, and Persians successively. Following an interval of Macedonian hegemony, Tarsus came under the Roman rule. After Ceasar's death, it became the land and the capital of Marc Anthony.

The Cleopatra gate

The ancient Tarsus was surrounded by three separate defense walls, with 12 meters of space between them. The gate by the sea, which is still standing today, is called the "Cleopatra gate."

The other works of art and ruins worth seeing near Tarsus. The most important among these are the Yedi Uyurlar Mağarası (The Seven Sleepers Cave), The Justinian Bridge, The Alexander Bath, The Roman Cave Cemeteries and the Ulucami Mosque which is an Ottoman mosque. built in the 16th century.

A D A N A

You travel further east from Tarsus, and soon you arrive in Adana, the fourth largest city of Turkey. The town has many attractions and sites that are worth visiting. The Regional Museum that contains a world famous collection of coins, reliefs of Hector and King Priam of Troy, the King's chariot and the Dragon, is a must see.

Other places of interest are the ruins of the Adana fortress, the Karatepe Museum containing Hittite remains, the Yılankale fortress near Ceyhan and the Anavarsa fortresses near Kozan.

Adana, stone bridge dating from the Roman era.

The Adna Archaeological Museum has an unparalleled collection of regional artifacts.

A N T A K Y A

You are now at the North-Eastern end of the Mediterranean Sea, and the Southernmost point of Turkey. On the way to Antioch, you have passed by the city of Alexandria, founded by Alexander the Great, but unfortunately there are no traces left behind from the ancient city.

As you walk through the Museum of Archeology, considered as one of the best in the world in terms of its mosaic collection, you will be amazed by the beauty and intricate patterns of the Roman Age mosaics, uncovered in the ancient city of Daphne. You can also visit the cave Church of St. Peter, one of the earliest churches in the history of Christianity, two kilometers away from the city.

Antakya, the Church of St. Peter.

Antakya, Water canals buit by Titus Vespianus.

Antakya Museum, interior view of the museum, which houses the world's most extensive collection of mosaics.

CENTRAL ANATOLIA

No matter where you start your travel in Turkey, either in Istanbul, İzmir, Antalya or any other city; if you have enough time, don't leave without spending a few days in Central Anatolia, especially in Cappadocia. Turkey is really a country to visit more than once; but what if you don't get the chance to come here again... It would be too bad that you missed all the beautiful spots you passed right by! The Central Anatolian plateau, 1000 meters high in average, and which stands like a bowl right between the mountains which surround it on all sides, will surprise you at first sight and give you the feeling that you are really far from home. This is a very different area with its seemingly never ending grain fields. its infinite plains, the green areas and poplar trees reminding you of the existence of water around here and its villages with dirt colored, straight roofs...

Ankara, (Anıtkabir) Mausoleum of Mustafa Kemal Atatürk.

A N K A R A

Ankara, known throughout the world for its Angora goats, was a small town of a population of 16,000, at the turn of this century. It was chosen as the strategic center of the country during the struggle for independence because Istanbul was occupied during the National War of Independence (1919-1922) and also because of other strategic reasons. Ankara remained the capital of Turkey after the Republic was founded in 1923. Ankara, which is Turkey's second largest city with its population of over 4 million today, is also under the pressure of rapid urbanization.

Yenişehir (new city) which is a good example of a modern city, and the squatter neighborhoods in which nearly half of the city reside are in sharp contrast with one another in Ankara.

The Museum of Anatolian Civilisations

Lovers of archeology should know that it is worth going to Ankara just to see the incredible collections in this museum. Besides the artifacts dating from the Upper Paleolithic Area found in the Karain cave in Antalya, the other very important representative of the Neolithic age are those excavated from the ancient city of Çatalhöyük. Archaeologists there uncovered unbelievably fine wall paintings, pottery and other fine artifacts and unbelievably beautiful artifacts from the bronze age. Thousands of artifacts are displayed here, those from the Assyrian trade colonies, the mighty Hittite Empire, and the Phrygian and Urartu civilizations. An Ottoman shopping area from the 15th century draws restaredinour day to be a museum the wide appreciation of all visitors.

Boğazköy, Rock Inscriptions and carvings - Hittite Sacred Area, Reliefs of the God Sharumma and King Tuthalia.

129

Hacı Bayram Mosque.

Ankara by night, Youth Park and Atatürk Mausoleum.

Ankara, Museum of Anatolian Civilizations: Twin Idol.

Hatti Woman Figurine.

Hittite Cult figuries and sun symbol.

The museum is next to the citadel, a Roman remain which has been repaired, restored, and changed very many times throughout its long history. After visiting the museum the visitor should wander through the citadel and breathe in the atmosphere of the 19th century Ankara houses. From the walls of the citadel the visitor gets to take in a panoramic view of the city below.

Temple of Augustus

This square is considered by all to be sacred. It is very special to the Moslem population as its includes the historical Hacı bayram Mosque which has been built adjacent to the ruins of this Roman temple. The walls and foundations of the ancient building can be clearly seen.

The Atatürk Mausoleum

The magnificent tomb of Mustafa Kemal Atatürk is evidence of the honor of which the memory of the commander of the Army for National Independence and the founder of the modern Republic of Turkey is held. This is definitely a place which any visitor to Ankara must visit. Make sure you also visit the small museum at the site.

Other places to visit in Ankara: Some other sites which should be visited by the visitor who has time are the Ethnographic Museum, the 30 hectar large Gençlik (youth) Parkı, the area around the Ulus Square, the modern city center of Kızılay and the boulevards that radiate to this center.

*Cappadocia,
Fairy Chimneys.*

CAPPADOCIA

What words can possibly be used to express or describe the area of Cappadocia? Shall we simply call it the eighth wonder of the world? Or that "miracle of Nature?" Or should we say that this is a geological event that became an unparalleled gift to the Anatolian lands? But whatever is said or written, it is not enough. For words themselves are not enable to describe the wonders of this place. This is truly one of the areas of the world which must, absolutely must, be seen, so make sure you don't miss this area on your visit to Turkey.

Millions of years ago the ancient volcanic mountains, chief among them the noble Erciyas, and the Hasan and Melendiz mountains, spread their volcanic ashes over the area. Time beat this ash down into a heterogenic tufa and

then for thousands upon thousands of years the winds blew and the rivers snaked through the lands and perhaps one of the most horrendous erosion events of all times became the geological miracle called Cappadocia.

The people of these immense valleys carved out immense hiding places for themselves, their animals, and their cities all, underground. Early Christians, too, used these underground sanctuaries to hide from the persecutions of the advancing Romans. Hermetic sects took to the hills and carved out chapels which they decorated with the finest of frescoes. And whole monasteries were carved out of hillsides. Habitats were also carved out and thousands of these hewn caves became snug homes as man merged with the Nature in which he resided. This is Cappadocia.

The visitor needs at least a week if

*Cappadocia,
detail of the
natural
formations.*

s/he is to explore every nook and cranny of the place, but one long day is enough to give the visitor an overview.

The Underground Cities

Cappadocia is along the trade route that joined the East with the West and the road taken by the Arab armies as they advanced against the Byzantines. It was for this reason that during the 7th through the 12th centuries AD the people of this area were under the constant threat of advancing armies. The Christians who inhabited these lands excavated two massive underground cities at Kaymaklı and Derinkuyu. Besides these two major cities there are a number of other, smaller towns and villages that had their "underground counterparts." These areas are truly underground "cities." Derinkuyu's city goes 12 floors underground and includes more than

Zelve, Interesting atmosphere of the Zelve Valley.

1200 rooms. In times of danger this underground haven could provide shelter to more than 10,000 people. Connected together by an underground road of 10 kilometers, the sister city of Kaymaklı has eight floors and the same number of rooms.

Rock Hewn Chapels

Probably the most interesting of the groupings of rock-hewn chapels is the open air museum of Göreme. Another is the series of chapels at the village of Çavuşin which are renown for their rich fresco designs. The region is literally packed with these kinds of chapels and other sacred areas carved out of the volcanic rock and then richly decorated. Unfortunately, certain Orthodox, influenced by the effects of Islam, called the Iconoclasts, began to destroy these images. This destruction of art lasted until

Paşabağ, Fairy Chimneys.

the 14th century. During this process, the kinds of decorations used on chapel walls changed radically. Today the original frescoes are being restored with a joint effort of the Ministry of Culture of the Turkish Republic and UNESCO. The frescoes in these chapels depict the lives of Christ and his followers and are described according to the beliefs of the Orthodox church.

The "Fortresses"

The people of the region did not only go underground when under the threat of an approaching army, they also carved immense "fortresses" out of the hills of volcanic tufa from which to defend their lands against the onslaught. The largest of these labyrinth type fortresses are those at Uçhisar, Ortahisar, and Sonhisar (Ürgüp). These areas are a photographer's delight as the region is dotted with the strange "fairy chimneys," rock-hewn houses, and pigeon holes.

Göreme, Open Air Museum, Elmalı (Apple) Church.

Göreme, Open Air Museum.

Typical views of Cappadocia.

Valleys

The Cappadocian lands are a series of valleys, among the most famous and the ones affording the most beautiful views are those of Ihlara (Peristrema), Zelve, Avcılar, Soğanlı, Derbent, Kılıçlar, Aşıklar, Güvercinlik, and Kızıl. But these are not all. There are at least 30 more valleys in the region, each offering something unique to see. Some have hermit chapels, while others have large churches hewn out of their rocky surfaces. Some have interesting fairy chimneys and others offer natural beauties, but all have historical sites and breathtaking nature that must be witnessed. The best way to take in the beauty of this incredible landscape is to walk. For those who want an easier way to get around, you can tour by horse or by donkey. There are even balloon tours available for the adventurous.

Nights in Cappadocia

If the weather is nice and the full moon is out, start your evening walk in the Red Valley and get a look at the deep red sunset which gives the valley its name. But don't stop there, continue on into the Derbent Valley, or another one. You will feel like you live in an unreal world and will be amazed with the views around you.

You will be surprised to see how one really and truly live in a dream world. We recommend you to visit one of the dozen lamb roasting restaurants in the area and have some local dry wine and watch the local folklore shows. Be sure to reserve your table in high season, otherwise you may not be able to find a seat!

Ürgüp.

Derinkuyu, Underground City.

K A Y S E R I

Kayseri was founded in the 2nd century B.C. by the Romans as Ceasareum and it is only 90 km away from the center of Cappadocia. Today, Kayseri is a city of more than 1 million people, where you will find many interesting things.

Kayseri is a beautiful and interesting city which has an airport providing faster access to Cappadocia and other ancient ruins in the region especially for tourists who have come to Turkey without a plan to visit Cappadocia.

For those who have time to spend in Kayseri, we suggest the following places to visit: the Castle with a medieval character which dates back to the 6th century and the Byzantine emperor Justinianus, the Huant Hatun Medresse an interesting example of Seljuk architecture which looks like a religious complex, Döner Kümbet, an extraordinary Seljuk monumental tomb, and the Archaeology Museum with its interesting collection.

Kayseri.

Whirling Dervishes.

Konya, Tomb of Mevlana (founder of the "Whirling Dervishes") and museum.

Konya, Interior View of Tomb of Mevlana.

K O N Y A

Like Kayseri, Konya was also founded by the Romans in the 2nd century as Iconium. Konya's population today is more than two million and it is the second largest city in central Anatolia after Ankara. Konya is full of interesting works early Turkish-Islamic architecture as the Anatolian Seljuk capital.

Certainly the Mevlana Museum is one of the most important places to visit in Konya. This small museum is next to a 16th century mosque which was built by Sinan during the Sultan Selim II period. This museum used to be Mevlana's lodge, the founder of the Whirling Dervishes.

This dervish lodge is visited by more than one million tourists every year as a result of Whirling Dervishes' fame around the world and it is definitely one of the most interesting places to visit in Konya. Mevlana's and Sultan Veled's tombs are near the museum. Many interesting artifacts used in the lodge, mystique musical instruments and many hand made rugs are exhibited in the lodge. You can also visit the cells of the Dervishes and the ethnographical section.

The following are the other places to visit in Konya: three medresse-museums from the Seljuk period with interesting architecture and beautiful tile and stone works: Karatay, Ince Minare and Sircali... The Alaeddin Mosque built by the Seljuk

Sultan Alaeddin Keykubat, the Archaeological Museum and the authentic old wheat bazaar...

The Eski Gümüş (old silver) Monastery near the city of Niğde is extraordinarily carved into the rocks. Sultanhan, the biggest caravanserai in Anatolia which was built in the 13th century is located on the Aksaray-Konya highway.

Ağzıkarahan is another large caravanserai located on the Aksaray-Nevsehir highway. The bird sanctuary close to Kayseri is one of the richest in the world.

The Salt Lake (Tuz Gölu) is the second largest salt lake in the world and Turkey's second largest lake and the Obruk lakes of central Anatolia located in the Konya plain are places worth visiting.

BOĞAZKÖY HATTUSAS

The first place to list here is the Hittite capital Hattusas, or Boğazkale, located 200 km away from Ankara. Hittites was the most important civilization in prehistoric Anatolia.

In the middle of wilderness, this extraordinary city resists the ravages of time alone on a plain and it is a visual feast for the visitor with its forts, city walls, temples and the remains of other settlements.

The Hittite sacred area Yazılıkaya would salute you with hundreds of Hittite gods if you go there at the right time with proper lighting -preferably around noon.

Boğazkale, Lion Gate, Gate to the capital of the Hittites.

Boğazköy, Yazılıkaya, Hittite Sacred Area.

Alacahöyük, Sphinx Gate.

BLACK SEA REGION

One of the most beautiful and greenest regions in Turkey, the Black Sea region has not attracted as much foreign or domestic tourism as it deserves. On the other hand, the western Black Sea coast is a peaceful vacation paradise starting at Ince Ada in Thrace, continuing at Kilyos, Sile, Karasu, Akçakoca, Amasra, Abana and Sinop.

Travelling east from Samsun, a combination of natural and historical beauty along with many ancient settlements is observed. This region gets the most rain in Turkey and it is a paradise where all different tones of green can be seen.   Let us continue our journey going north from Ankara and visit the Hittite cities Hattusas and Yazılıkaya and if you have time, Alacahöyük. We will turn left and give a short break in Amasya before we reach the Black Sea shore in Samsun.

Amasya.

A M A S Y A

Traveling 322 km from Ankara towards Samsun, you reach Amasya. This beautiful city which was on the Silk Road between Istanbul and Iran is worth getting to know. The city is located on both sides of the Yeşilırmak river at a narrow point and it leans against steep rocks where a Hellenistic castle was located. The royal tombs carved into the rocks from the Pontus era are immediately noticed. Called Amaseia then, the city was an important cultural and commercial center. This city has attracted the attention of many civilizations throughout history and is the birthplace of Strabon , the renowned geographer.

After the Pontus kingdom, the city was ruled by the Romans, Byzantines, Arabs, Armenians and Seljuks after the 11th century, Mongolians during the great invasion, and finally the Ottomans. After Yıldırım Bayezid was defeated by Tamerlane in 1402, his son Mehmed I made Amasya a defensive base and resisted the Mongolians attacks there.

At the entrance to the city, the citadel on a hilltop and rock tombs are seen. On the right of Yeşilırmak (ancient Iris) is the Torumtay tomb.

The Gök Medresse and Mosque were built by Torumtay in the 13th century during the period of the Seljuk Sultan Alaeddin Keyhüsrev and are located next to the tomb. The 15th century Yorguc Pasha Mosque and Bayezid II Mosque are also worth visiting.

The Aynalı Cave dates back to the Hellenistic ages and is located 2 km north of town.

We shall continue our trip towards the Black Sea.

The Black Sea, Sinop.

*Giresun,
Tirebolu
Fortress.*

*Fatsa,
Haznedaroğlu
Residence.*

*Two typical
scenes of the
Black Sea.*

O R D U
G I R E S U N

After Samsun, which is a nice, big town with good hotels, you travel east for about 170 km on a scenic road and reach Ordu. Called Cotyora in ancient times, Ordu was founded by merchants from Sinop in the 5th century B.C. The oldest building in town today is a basilica from the 17th century.

As you continue east from Ordu, you reach Giresun after 50 km. The city was founded by the Pontus king Pharmas during the 2nd century B.C. and was called Pharmacia then. It was named after the fruit Coresus, cherry, later. The Roman commander Lucullus had cherries for the first time here and liked them very much.

He sent the cherry saplings to Rome and introduced cherries to the western world. You notice a small island as you exit the town: ancient Aretias.

According to the legend, two Amazon queens, Ortrez and Antiope were sacrificed for the god Mars -Ares- on this island. You arrive in Trabzon after traveling 140 km.

TRABZON

Similar to Ordu, Trabzon, too, was founded by the merchants from Sinope around 1,000 B.C. and today it is the most important city in the region. It leans with its back against the Eastern Black Sea mountains and it is an important port city. The city is famous for its natural and historical treasures. The famous historian Xenophon got lost and arrived in Trapezos (which means table or plain in old Greek) with the remainder of his 10,000 soldiers. He says that the local people were really happy to see them. The city has strategic importance since it is located at the beginning of the road that connects Black Sea coast to Iran and is right by the famous Zigana pass. Trabzon was, therefore, of strategic importance and considered a rich prize by many. Luluctuc conquered the city during the Roman times, but the city managed to retain its "independent" status. Ruled by the Goths for a short time, the city then became an important citadel for the Byzantines. Justinianus the Great rebuilt the city walls. The Seljuks tried to take over the city several times but were never successful. When Istanbul was invaded by the Latins during the 4th Crusade, the Byzantine dynasty moved to Iznik. The two sons of the emperor come to Trabzon and Alexios Comnenos becomes the emperor here. In 1461, the city entered under Ottoman rule.

The St. Sophia church is the most important historical building in Trabzon, which is today a center of commerce and tourism. The first church built by the Comnenos family in the 13th century was expanded later by emperor Manuel

Trabzon, Hagia Sophia Church.

Paleologos VIII in the same century. The church was converted into a mosque in the 16th century and was converted into a museum in 1957. Some faint frescoes are still noticeable inside.

There are several other important Byzantine churches which were converted to mosques and are worth seeing for their interesting architecture. Phanagia Chrysocephalos Church (Fatih Mosque), Saint Eugene church (Yeni Cuma Camii), Saint Anne and Saint Basil churches are some of those.

Trabzon, Frescoes, Hagia Sophia Church.

Trabzon, Maçka, The Monastery of the Mother Mary.

Trabzon, Two interior views, Monastery of the Mother Mary.

S U M E L A

However the most important site in Trabzon is the Sumela Monastery. The monastery is located above a valley inside the Pontic mountains and is reached after a pleasant ride with

beautiful views of nature. After the last point that can be reached by car, a strenuous hike up the hill starts. As you get closer, you feel like you are about to experience something unreal.

The monastery looks like it has been taken down from the sky and pasted on the side of the hill.

No one has been able to answer the question of how mankind was able to build such a huge monastery on the wall of a mountain with the technology of the 6th century. 14th century additions to Sumela gave it its final look today and it definitely is one of the most significant tourist attractions on Turkey.

As you look at the frescoes on the walls in the monastery (unfortunately, in bad condition), do not forget to drink some cold water from the sacred spring.

Sis Mountains, Women in traditional dress at a meadow festivals.

Black Sea, Woman selling goods at the market.

Uzungöl.

EASTERN ANATOLIA REGION

Leaving Trabzon, you have two options to discover the nature and history in the Eastern Anatolia region: either you can travel across the Zigana pass (2,400m.) and Kop pass (2,500m) and arrive in Erzurum, or if you have time, you can follow the Black Sea coast towards the east, go through Rize and Artvin and reach the north-east corner of Turkey. At this point, you are alongside the Çoruh river, considered to be one of the best rafting areas in the world. Around the Yusufeli area, you can visit several Georgian churches which represent an interesting architectural character.

E R Z U R U M

Located 2,000 meters above sea level, Erzurum is like an open air museum with the abundance of historical buildings.

The city was built as Theodosiopolis by the Byzantines.

In 622, it was the home of a council who pressured the Armenians to join the Orthodox church; he was not successful.

The emperor Constantinus V exiled the local people to Thrace for the same reason, but he was not successful in persuading the Armenians to become Orthodox, either.

Having been ruled by the Arabs, the Armenian Bagratides and the Abbasids, the city was conquered by the Seljuks in 1049 and its name was changed to Arz el Rum. Among many places to see in Erzurum, the most important ones are

Yakutiye Medresse built by Ilhan Olcayto and a Mongolian governor in the 14th century, significant for its outer decoration and stonework, Çifte Minareli Medresse which was started during the Alaattin Keykubad period and finished after his death, Hatuniye Medresse and the tomb next to it, the Ulu Cami (Great Mosque) which was built by Alaeddin Keyhüsrev with seven naves and two domes, the Emir Sultan Tomb and the museum in which more than ten thousand artifacts are exhibited.

p.51: Erzurum, Three "Kümbets" (memorial tombs) dating from the Seljuk era.

Erzurum, Yakutiye Medresse.

Erzurum, Çifte Minareli (Twin Minarets) Mosque.

K A R S

The initial settlement date is not known, but Kars gained its importance in history as it became the capital for the Bagratid family in the 10th century. Kars remained as an important place even after the Bagratid capital was moved to Ani. Ruled by the Seljuks in the 11th century and taken over by the Georgians in the 13th century, the city joined the Ottoman empire in the 16th century, like the rest of eastern Anatolia.

Kars was under Russian rule between 1878 and 1917 and some urban planning was done in the city at that time. Kars, therefore, resembles a typical Russian cities. The wide cobblestone roads and perpendicular streets provide easier transportation in the city.

The 16th century citadel, the 11th century Armenian church and Kars Museum are worth seeing.

A N I

Arpaçay is the border between Armenia in the easternmost point in Turkey, adjacent to the Ani ruins. The Ani ruins are the most important site to see in the Kars region. Ani kept its strategic importance all the time since it was built as a passage between Anatolia and Asia. When it became the capital of the Bagratids by the king Ashot III, the city was rebuilt and two rows of city walls were built around it. The city has eight entrances. The Alp Arslan Gate is used to enter the settlement and the view is really magnificent! Straight ahead one can see the Armenian border towers. The inner fortress which was built in the 7th century is still intact.

The Great Cathedral is significant with its cruciform plan, three naves and domes; the outside of the cathedral is decorated with carvings and stone work

Kars, One of the churches built by the Russians during their occupation of the city.

is excellent. In the east of the city is the church of St. Gregory. It was built in the 13th century with a cruciform plan and it was covered with a conical dome. There are carvings on the outside and frescoes inside the church.

The remains of two mosques, a caravanserai and a large bath can also be visited here.

A Ğ R I

One of the border towns on the eastern part of Turkey, Ağrı was also strategically important. Ruled by the Mitannis, Hurri, Urartians, Armenians, Persians, Arabs, Byzantines, Seljuks and Ottomans.

Ağrı is also home for the highest mountain in Turkey. The name of the city comes from Ararat, mentioned in the Old Testament.

Kars, Ani, Cathedral of Ani.

The Church of St. Gregory.

Mt. Ararat (Ağrı Dağı)

The first book of Old Testament says: "Noah's Arc landed on top of Mt. Ararat on the seventeenth day of the seventh month". It is the highest mountain in Turkey (5,165 meters). This huge mass with 30 km around it is all in the Turkish soil. The mountain can be viewed from Iran and Armenia, as well. The last activity of this old volcano was in 1840. The first Christians in Anatolia are believed to have lived inside the caves at 2,100 meters. The carved crucifixes can still be seen on the walls of these caves. In the north-east part of the mountain is the largest glacier in Turkey above 3,100 meters. The Yakut Spring close by is believed to be the source where everybody who got off Noah's Arc drank water for the first time. The Kup Lake is located at 4,000 meters. The ruins of an Armenian church and the Horan Citadel are located close by.

Doğubeyazıt, İshak Pasha Palace.

Climbed for the first time by Frederic Parrot in 1829, many mountaineers climbed to the top of Mt. Ararat, some looking for the remains of Noah's Ark. So far, nothing has been found related to the Noah's Ark.

DOĞUBEYAZIT

This town is close to the Iranian border and is famous for the Ishak Pasha Palace in the center of the old city.

Ishak Pasha Palace

Mount Ararat, the highest point of the Anatolian plateau.

The palace was built by Ishak Pasha, the governor of the region in 1784. Since the area is hilly, a total area of 7,600 square meters had to be prepared and leveled for the construction of the palace. The palace was made by using red clay stones and it resembles the Topkapı and Edirne palaces. Its high minaret can be seen from far away. All the buildings in the town of Doğubeyazıt which surrounds the palace were destroyed during an earthquake. The palace is entered through a door that resembles the Seljuk style arch doors. The first courtyard is the palace security courtyard and the stalls and warehouses are located here. The second courtyard is entered through a Gothic style door. On the right is the mosque which is quite large compared to the size of the palace. The mosque with a single minaret and a dome displays great stonework. The tomb next to the mosque belongs to Ishak Pasa's parents. The largest part of the palace is the harem which was built on two floors. There are many rooms, halls and baths in this building. A central heating system was formed by passing the hot water from the baths through pipes inside the walls.

V A N

Van is one of the most important cities of the old Vaspurakan region. It is located on the east coast of Lake Van and its ancient name is Tooshpa. 1,700 meters above sea level, the winter lasts for six months in this town. In a short time during the Urartian period, a large, highly civilized city was established in the area. The Urartians got weak as a result of Scythian and Cimmerian attacks in the 7th century, and by the 6th century they fell under the rule of the Medes. Later, Persians, Alexander, Pontus Kingdom, Seleukos, Romans, Byzantines, Armenians, Seljuks and, starting in the 16th century, Ottomans ruled the area.

Van Citadel

It was built by the Urartian king Sardur I, by the lake. The old town of Tooshpa next to the citadel was later flooded by the lake destroying most of the evidence from the Armenian, Seljuk and Ottoman periods.

Of the few ruins that can be visited are the 13th century Ulu Cami and Kızıl Cami mosques.

Toprakkale, 5 km east of the city became the capital during the period of the Urartian king Rasutina. The artifacts found during the excavations show us how civilized the Urartians were.

The most important of these findings are exhibited at the Anatolian Civilizations Museum in Ankara, the ones with second degree of importance are in Van Museum.

Çavuştepe

This settlement was excavated after the Turkish republic was founded and it provides us with more detailed ideas

Van, General view of the Urartian fortress.

View from the Citadel of Old Van.

Van, Ahlat, Two "Kümbets" (memorial tombs) dating from the Suljuk period.

Emir Bayındır Kümbet, one of the "Twin Kümbets."

158

about the Urartian civilization. The inscriptions found tell us that the city was founded by Sardur II and was made the capital.

A temple dedicated to the God Haldi, houses, storage areas and city walls were unearthed. The Urartian alphabet was used in the inscriptions.

Hoşab Kalesi
This magnificent citadel is located on top of a hill by the town of Güzelsu on Van-Başkale highway. It was built by Sarı Süleyman, a Mahmudi ruler in 1643. The writing above the door tells us about its history.

Van, Lake Van, Ahtamar Island and the Church.

160

AKDAMAR ISLAND

Akdamar is a small island which is 4km from the coast on the Van-Tatvan highway, several kilometers past Gevas. The small Akdamar church built by Vaspurakan king Gagik I in the 10th century is a masterpiece. It is the work of architect Manuel.

Red clay stone was used in the construction of this church and it has domes, a cruciform plan, and three entrances.

A chapel in the 13th century and a large front section in the 14th century were added to the church. The Armenian Patriarchy was moved here in the 10th century.

The outside walls are decorated with scenes from the Old Testament, and these figures look like sculptures under the sunlight. In the shade, these figures seem almost to disappear. The inside walls of the church have frescoes depicting scenes from the bible.

A Byzantine influence is clearly seen in the wall pictures, even though some of them are badly ruined.

Van, Hoşab Fortress.

DIYARBAKIR

As you travel west from Van, you can either go south or north of Lake Van. Either way, you get to Tatvan and from here continue towards Diyarbakır. 26 km after Tatvan, you pass through a small but interesting town: Bitlis. An Armenian trade center in the medieval ages, the Kurds ruled the town in the 16th century. Later, the town was ruled by the Ottomans.

If you have enough time in Bitlis, you can take a look at the 12th century Ulu Camii and 16th century Seref Camii and Medresse. Then you will go through Silvan. Being on the main road to Mesopotamia made Silvan important in history. At first, it was called Mayafirikin and later the name was changed to Martyrapolis. Patriarch Marutha gathered a council in the 5th century and he convinced the Persian king Yezgered I to allow Christianity to be introduced in the region. The most important historical building in Silvan is the 13th century Ulu Cami.

Finally, you arrive in Diyarbakir after a long journey. We know from the excavations completed that there were civilizations dating back to 7,000 B.C. in the area. The city was ruled by the Mitanni, Hurri, Assryians, Urartians, Persians, Romans, Byzantines, Arabs, Seljuks and Ottomans, respectively. The old name of the city was Amida, originated from the Persians. The massive basalt city walls built by Constanz in the 4th century can still be seen. The aerial view of the city walls resembles a fish.

The walls are one of the most important military buildings today dating back to the medieval ages. The walls are rectangularly shaped and have rounded corners; these walls extend 1,300 meters in the north-south and 1,700 meters in

Three scenes from Diyarbakır (the largest city in South-Eastern Anatolia): View of Diyarbakır from the walls of the citadel, Folk Dancers, Inside the City.

Urfa, Halil-ül Rahman Mosque and Balıklı (fish) Lake.

the east-west direction. The city walls are 3 to 5 meters thick and 10 to 12 meters high. It has four main gates: Harput in the north, Yeni in the east, Mardin in the south and Urfa in the west. There are 80 towers on the city walls.

The places worth seeing in Diyarbakir are listed as follows: Ulu Cami, which was converted into a mosque from a church in the 7th century by the Arabs who conquered the city. The Sunni Islam's four main "Hak" sects (Shiism is not considered to be a Hak sect), Hanefilik, Malikilik, Hanbelilik and Safiilik are represented in different prayer rooms in this mosque which shows a unique architectural character as a synthesis of different styles. The Zincirli Medresse from the 7th century, the 16th century Peygamber Mosque can also be visited. Besides, the Ottoman bridge on Tigris is worth a visit.

U R F A

Using a shortcut from Diyarbakır, Urfa can be reached via Siverek and Hilvan. If you have time, we suggest you extend your travels somewhat to take in the exciting city of Mardın. This city, called Marida in days of old, is very interesting with its buildings constructed of pastel colored natural stone. The city was built on a hill top affording a bird's eye view of the Mesopotamian plain extending below. All of the homes have flat roofs, giving this city a typical South-Eastern Anatolian appearance. Of special note in the city are the Ulu Cami (grand mosque) and the Medresse (now used as a museum) which date from the the eleventh century Saltık Principality. Ten kilometers out of the city is Deyrülzafara, the monastery of the Assyrian order. This complex is definitely worth seeing.

Urfa has been called "the city of prophets." This town has witnessed all of the history of Anatolia. Called "Edesse" in the time of Alexander the Great, it was occupied by the Seljuk Turks in the eleventh century. It was ruled by four French counts during the Crusades (1098-1146) and fell to the Ottomans in the sixteenth century. It was during this period that the name of the city was changed to "Ruha."

It is believed that this city was the home of five different prophets and that the prophet Abraham was born in a cave in the city. The old fortress remaining to this day dates from the Crusades. The fortress is surrounded by moats on three of its sides, while the fourth is backed against a sharp cliff. The cave of the prophet is called today the "Halil İbrahim Cave," and local people believe the water in the cave is sacred.

The cave of the Moslem holy man, Eyüp, is six kilometers outside of town on the road to Akçakale. One steps down five steps to enter the cave and they are believed to be a symbol of the patience of the holy man who spent seven years in isolation.

Balıklı Göl

This man-made lake was formed by joining the Halil-ül Rahman and Ayn-El Zeliha lakes by canals. The carp which swim in the lake are believed to be sacred. The Halil-ül Rahman and Rızvaniye Mosques are also worth seeing.

View of Urfa from the Urfa Citadel.

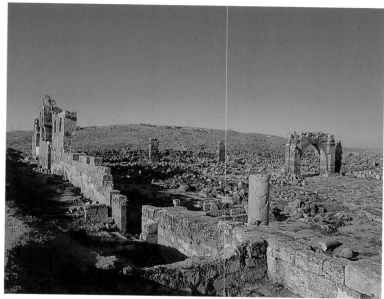

H A R R A N

35 kilometers from the Akçakale you turn towards Doğulu, after another nine kilometers you find yourself in the highly interesting town of Harran. The first thing to strike your eyes is a collection of mud-brick buildings with cone and dome shaped roofs that are scattered over the dry plains. This placed known as Carh in history is of great importance. The Sim cult, which was one of the two main Mesopotaimian civilizations settled and developed in this area. Stars and planets were very important in the Sim beliefs. The Sim people also worshipped the moon. It is known that the famous Sim temple was in Harran, but unfortunately there are no remains left today. During the Roman period, the famous Caracalla, much under the influence of this belief cult, urged that the religion be attached to the Roman palace. Mark Anthony refused and had Caracalla executed.

Interesting scenes from Harran.

M O U N T   N E M R U T

Alexander the Great, the Emperor of the World, moved through Anatolia in the 4th century BC, after he conquered Macedonia and other regions, in order to free the Anatolian people from the Persian rule.

This date marks the beginning of the Hellenistic period. Alexander the Great had the ideal of becoming the Emperor of the whole world, and so also thought about mixing the races. He forced thousands of soldiers and officers to marry the women of the areas they conquered.

As a result of this, the Commagene Kingdom was formed between 1st century BC and 1st century AD in the area that is known as Adıyaman today and a mixed Hellen/Persian peoples emerged. Antiochos I, the most important king of this civilization, built himself a monumental tumulus grave on Mount Nemrut (2100 m.), one of the largest mountains in the area.

The tumulus was made of little stones and was about 50 m. high. Antiochos I had the surrounding area decorated like a temple and added statues of gods, which had heads two-meters high.

The fact that he had his own statue built, along with the likes of Apollo, Fortuna, Hercules and Zeus, shows that he saw himself as a divinity.

Mount Nemrut which is called the 8th Wonder of the World by some has a certain kind of mystery that enchants everyone who sees it.

Nemrut. Unforgettable view: the head of the God Apollo at sunset.

Nemrut. View of the Eastern terrace. Head of Zeus is in the forefront.